Prisoner of Her Culture

Sakina's

Fight for freedom

Randy L. Noble

Front cover photograph courtesy of

Dreamstime.com

"The education and empowerment of women throughout the world cannot fail to result in a more caring, tolerant, just, and peaceful life for all..."

Aung San Suu Kyi

1991 winner of the Nobel Prize for peace

"Sire! What use is this black chador to me?

A thousand mercies, why do you reward me with this?

I am not in mourning that I should wear this, to flag my grief to the world...

I am not a disease that needs to be drowned in secret darkness......

Chadur and Char-diwari

Fahmida Riaz...Pakistani poet

"Let us pick up our books and our pens; they are our most powerful weapons.

One child, one teacher, one book and one pen can change the world..."

Malala Yousafzai

"Malala day," United Nations speech, July 2013

Dedications

To the very special women in my life who have made the world a better place to live in because of their contributions............

Becky Noble

My multi-talented wife Becky speaks out for our freedoms through the many conservative blogs and news articles that she writes for The Blacksphere.net and also her weekly radio broadcast, "The Conservative Cauldron," on Blog Talk Radio.

Zainab Khan.

Zainab is a very influential activist for the rights of women through her public speaking and incredible paintings. She is featured in the powerful documentary film, "Honor Diaries," that exposes the horrific abuses committed against women in Muslim-majority countries in the Middle East.

Nahren Anweya

Nahren has dedicated her life to being a voice for the suffering Assyrian Christians in Iraq and works tirelessly for their human rights as they struggle to survive against genocide and ethnic cleansing.

Paymaneh Sabet

Paymaneh is a beautiful and passionate Iranian Christian refugee living in Malaysia. She writes excellent human rights articles for my radio program, "The Cross in the desert." She is committed to the freedom of her people who live under the oppression and fear of the Iranian government.

"Cultural acceptance does not mean accepting the unacceptable. It's about time we put an end to laws and norms that support the violence perpetrated against women in the name of culture or religion...."

Zainab Khan.

Human rights activist from the documentary, "Honor Diaries."

PREFACE

Farzana Parveen was guilty of breaking her family's "code of honor." At 25, she was now pregnant and had bravely decided to go against the wishes of her family by marrying a man of her own choice. Accused of abduction by her family, Farzana arrived at the courthouse in Lahore to defend her husband. Twenty of her family members were waiting and after her arrival, they fired gunshots and began beating her. The violence quickly escalated and they began throwing bricks at her. In just a matter of moments, Farzana lay dead in a pool of blood, brutally stoned to death, in broad daylight before a frightened crowd of onlookers.

Asia Bibi hasn't seen her husband and children in more than five years. Appeal after appeal has been turned down by the Lahore High Court as Pakistan continues to uphold the death sentence against Asia for blasphemy.

Asia lives in a country where Islamic extremists are extremely harsh against Christians and often times uses the "blasphemy law" against them with discriminatory motives. In June of 2009, Asia was busy working with a group of Muslim women harvesting berries. She was accused of drinking from the same water bowl as them, which is considered unclean because she is a Christian. A brief confrontation ensued and Asia was accused of insulting the Prophet Mohammed, which is punishable by death in Pakistan.

Both Farzana and Asia are victims of an unjust system of oppressive laws that discriminates against women in Pakistan. Honor killings, public stoning's, and acid attacks happen far too frequently in a country where the wishes of a family are elevated above human choices. The Human Rights commission of Pakistan documented more than 913 honor killings in 2013, 99 of them committed against minors. Human life is not upheld and respected by the law, who often turn their backs and turn a deaf ear to the cries of the oppressed.

In 2014, a powerful documentary film entitled, "Honor Diaries," broke the silence and became a voice for the rights of women in Muslim-majority countries where the gruesome acts of Female genital mutilation and honor killings take place. Muslim activist women bravely took to the public platform denouncing these horrible practices and calling for a reform to all of the unjust laws. One of the participants in the film, Zainab Khan, has been a frequent guest on my radio program, "The Cross in the desert." Zainab engages in public speaking and uses her talents in painting as a vehicle for promoting what she calls, "visual activism." She is a gifted human rights activist and artist, courageously promoting *gender equality,* standing up for the rights of oppressed women in Middle Eastern cultures that suffer under "male domination."

In my previous publications, I have taken up the cause of speaking out for the oppressed women in Iran. After watching, "Honor Diaries," I felt compelled to take up the cause of Pakistani women. I have shared my radio programs and books with my "Facebook" friends all over the world of the internet in order to be a "voice for the voiceless!" There is a risk in breaking the silence. The brave women of "Honor Diaries" have put their lives and reputations at risk in order to rescue women from becoming more victims and statistics in the headline news!

I join with the brave women of "Honor Dairies" in my latest publication to bring awareness to the plight of women living in Pakistan. If we fail to speak out, there will be more women like Farzana and Asia whose lives will be tragically altered by societies that exalt honor over choice. The time is short and there is an urgent need to speak out now. The Bible commands us to be a "voice for the voiceless."

"Speak up for those who cannot speak for themselves: ensure justice for those being crushed. Yes, speak up for the poor and helpless and see that they get justice!"

(Proverbs 31:8-9)

Dedicated to the brave voice from Pakistan:

Malala Yousafzai

"One book and one pen can change the world!"

"Let us take up our books and pens, for they are our most powerful weapons!"

All of us at one time or another have been inspired and motivated by famous speeches.

Abraham Lincoln's powerful Gettysburg Address in 1863 in which he lamented the bloody cost of the Civil War, contains the unforgettable phrase, *"that government of the people, by the people and for the people, will never perish from the earth."*

Or who can forget, JKF's speech that challenged all Americans with the famous question, *"Ask not what your country can do for you, ask what you can do for your country."*

Finally, the late Dr. Martin Luther King, in the midst of the bloody struggle for racial equality in 1963, declared to a nation torn apart by racism, *"I have a dream!"*

Words are very powerful! Words can change the destiny of our lives.......

Recently I was inspired and challenged by the words of Malala Yousafzai, who gave a powerful, life-changing speech at the United Nations on her 16th birthday. On October 6, 2012 Malala was seriously wounded after being shot in the head by the Taliban in her native country of Pakistan. Nearly one year later after many surgeries in the UK and Pakistan, Malala made a miraculous recovery.

On July 12, 2013, on her 16th birthday, Malala Addressed the United Nations Assembly in what I believe was one of the most courageous speeches that I've ever heard. With her mother and father present, Malala, dressed in a beautiful pink and white hijab, stood at the podium, thanking everyone for their prayers and praising the doctors and nurses for her astonishing recovery.

"I speak not for myself, but for those without a voice so they can be heard," Malala declared.

She then recalled the frightening day when she was shot and made a bold declaration saying, *" They thought that the bullet would silence us, but they failed, out of that silence came thousands of voices!"*

There was a rousing applause and then Malala boldly proclaimed, "The terrorists thought they would change my aim and stop my ambition, but nothing changed except weakness, fear and hopelessness died and strength and courage was born! I don't hate the Taliban that shot me!"

Malala credited Mohammed and Jesus for teaching her compassion and her parents for impressing on her the importance of forgiveness.

"Extremists are afraid of books and pens," Malala pointed out as she urged the governments of the world to help her wage war against illiteracy, poverty and terrorism. Malala's goal is to ensure and protect the rights of every woman and every child across the globe through peace and education.

"Let us take up our books and pens. They are our most powerful weapons!"

I watched this speech in tears! I was so proud and inspired by this young girl's courage! When I think about the role models for our teenagers today, Malala is the first person who comes to my mind! She is my hero! We need more role models like Malala instead of the "hip-hop" celebrities who are busy promoting drugs and sex and leading many of our teens down the road to ruin.

After watching her speech, I'm sure you will agree with me that one day we will see Malala as the next woman president of Pakistan!

"He looked down from earth to heaven, to hear the groans of the prisoners, to release those condemned to die...."

(Psalm 102:20)

"Bring me out of prison, that I may give thanks to your name."

(Psalm 142:7)

Chapter One

Sakina the brick maker

The bright rays of the noon-day sun beat down upon the pile of moist clay laying in the palms of Sakina's hands. It was another blistering hot day in the brick making kiln of Pakistan. Sakina was bent down low in a squatting position toward the ground. For almost tens hours a day, five days a week, Sakina endured the hot sun and the intense pain of squatting down making bricks to earn money and help pay off her father's loan.

Beads of sweat streamed down her face as she carefully rolled the hot clay skillfully in her hands, much like preparing dough for baking fresh bread. The next step in brick making was placing the moist clay into a steel rectangular molder, spreading it carefully into each corner, shaping it into a perfectly designed brick. Once she had fitted the clay perfectly into the molder, she then pressed it down firmly with both of her hands and turned it upside down. A new brick had been created and placed alongside a long row of other bricks forming a long assembly line.

The process of brick making was both back breaking and grueling. Every day Sakina awoke at sunrise, eating a quick breakfast, consisting of tea and rice and traveled with her father and two brothers to the city of Mandi Bahauddin in the Punjab province of Pakistan. Sakina was born in the village of Shaheedan Wali, a farming community consisting of wheat, rice and sugar cane plants. It was a 35 minute bus ride to the city of Mandi Bahauddin that Sakina endured almost every day. Her father Akbar was a seasoned carpenter who barely made enough to support his family. Struggling to make ends meet, he had borrowed some money from Mustafa, the land owner of the brick making kiln. Mustafa was a stern task master. He had a reputation of abusing young children who worked at the kiln. Pakistan was notorious for forced child laborers who lived like slaves, sweating in the hot sun every day, sometimes for 14 hours, making bricks for the kiln.

The child laborers worked in a filthy, unsanitary environment with few breaks and very little food. Each child barely made enough to survive, earning little more than 200 rupees a day, which is equivalent to $3.50 in American money.

Sakina endured the hot sun each day, dressed in Shalwar Kameez, the traditional clothes of a woman living in Pakistan. The Shalwar consisted of pajama-like trousers, the legs wide at the top and narrow at the ankle. The Kameez was a long shirt or tunic, that draped down over the Shalwar trousers. Sakina also wore a dupatta, a silk scarf that was fashionably draped across her shoulders just below the neck. Besides the dupatta and kameez, Sakina also wore a hijab covering her hair, a requirement for Muslim women when going out publicly amongst men.

Sakina reached over to the pile of clay lying next to her. There was a precise system to brick making that began with a group of younger boys breaking the soil with a hoe and putting it into a wheelbarrow. After filling the wheelbarrow with the moist clay, one of the boys would hurriedly transport it to where Sakina was working and empty the pile of clay down next to her.

After Sakina had molded bricks for four hours, carefully stacking them in several rows, the bricks would then be transported to the kiln where they were heated up in the fire of a burning oven to finally become the finished brick that would be used in the construction of a house.

Taking the clay in her hands, she carefully rolled it for a few seconds and then laid it down in the steel molder *(shaped like a shoe box)* to form and fashion it into the shape of a brick. Bending over in a stopped position to mold bricks all day in the hot sun was agonizing. Sakina's body ached and her knees were stiff from squatting for hours. By the end of a long day, Sakina was in excruciating pain. There were only two breaks in the 10 hour days, one at noon and one at 3 pm for a brief lunch snack. By noon time, Sakina was already exhausted and covered in sweat.

Sakina paused from her labor and wiped the sweat from around the silk band of her hijab that covered her hair and part of her forehead. Her mind drifted back to Sunday, just two days ago when she celebrated her 11th birthday! Sakina smiled with joy and remembered how grateful she was to her father for letting her have the day off to celebrate. Akbar was a stern and disciplined man, committed to raising his children to strict adherence to the teachings of the Quran.

Sakina peered down toward her chest, running her fingers softly over the edges of the silk blue dupatta that her father had surprised her with on her birthday. Blue was Sakina's favorite color, matching her deep beautiful blue eyes. She was thrilled that her father had blessed her with a wonderful birthday present. She managed to smile, but then quickly looked down toward the ground in despair. It was very difficult to be close to Akbar. Sakina feared her father. At times he was very abusive to her. Yet unfortunately, it was something she had grown up to accept.

In Pakistan, the birth of a male is preferred to that of a female in order to carry on the family name. Sakina felt cursed to be born a female. She felt worthless and unwanted, being consistently reminded that a woman's place is in the home. Women in Pakistan were taught to be submissive and silent having no voice in society. In Pakistan, women were considered the property of males. They were treated as a commodity that can be exchanged, bought or sold. A woman could be handed over to an adversary as blood money in order to settle a tribal conflict.

The intense heat was beginning to overwhelm Sakina. She was exhausted and drenched in sweat. Stacking the last brick down on the top of the row, Sakina stood up from her squatting position. It was finally break time. She was allowed two breaks per shift. One half-hour break for lunch and one 15 minute afternoon break. It was 3 pm. Quitting time was in two hours when she would meet up with her brothers, Abdul and Hassan, and they would walk together to the bus stop. Akbar was always prompt.

He would meet them there at 5 pm, expecting his children to be on time.

Taking a deep breath, Sakina relaxed from the excruciating, back breaking work of laboring in the sun. She looked down the gravel road that led to a small grove of trees. In the grove of trees was an old pump water fountain, which was the perfect place for taking a break. Sakina hurried down the road realizing that the other children would be there soon also and then there would be a fight for the water fountain.

After a short walk, Sakina arrived at the old rusted-out water fountain. She couldn't believe that she was all alone. Her throat was dry and parched from the intense heat. Stepping up to the fountain, Sakina pressed down on the steel pad with her foot and immediately a stream of cold, refreshing water gushed out. She leaned over and let the water splash and wash all over her face. It was a welcomed exhilarating feeling, cold water gently soothing and washing the dirt and dust off her dry and parched skin.

Sakina paused and held out the palms of her hands, catching the stream of water and then splashing it across her face.

"Get back to work!"

The sound of an angry voice startled Sakina. She quickly lifted her foot from off of the steel pedal and spun around. In the distance she could see Mustafa, the kiln landlord, pushing a young child with both of his hands in a fit of rage. The young boy burst into tears, crying in fear.

" You lazy bastard!" Mustafa yelled and then sternly kicked the young child in the back with his foot. The boy screamed in agony, falling down on the ground.

Sakina turned away in fear. She couldn't watch any longer. Mustafa was a cruel and abusive landlord. He had a reputation of treating the young children harshly and at times, physically abusing them. Sakina was gripped with fear. She quickly hid behind one of the tree trunks afraid that Mustafa would see her. She began to tremble. Tears filled her eyes. Abuse, fear, murder and rape, perfectly described her country. Pakistan was a nation with a troubled past filled with violence, turmoil, murder and greed. 1947 was a pivotal date in Pakistan's history. They had split from British-occupied India and declared themselves a sovereign nation. The Muslims had been seeking a homeland free from discrimination and persecution by the Hindus in India. Yet turmoil and violence followed the new country. Muslims consistently fought with one another. Politics, corruption, and assassinations hung like dark clouds over the new nation.

Now just two days after her 11th birthday on October 5, the United States had invaded Afghanistan in hot pursuit of Osama Bin Laden and the Taliban to exact revenge for the terrorist attacks in New York City. Sakina was filled with apprehension and anxiety. What if the United States also invaded her country? She had heard on the news that Osama Bin Laden might be hiding out in the mountains.

Mustafa finally left the crying young boy alone after emotionally and physically humiliating him. Watching him crawl on the ground in the distance, Sakina wept with compassion for him. She could almost feel his pain and the bruises all over his tiny body.

After a few moments, she composed herself and looked down next to the tree trunk. Her eyes widened with joy as she gazed at two beautiful wildflowers in full bloom. Pakistan was known for its beautiful array of flowers. One type of wildflower was the bright and elegant yellow dandelion. Sakina marveled at its beautiful bright yellow array of petals. Suddenly the ugliness and cruelty of the brickmaking kiln had been magically transformed by a pair of fragrant and beautiful wildflower dandelions. Sakina knelt down and gently broke the stem of one of the dandelions and lifted it up to her nose. She closed her eyes and inhaled the tantalizing fragrance of the dandelion. In her mind's eye, she could visualize herself running free in a field of wildflowers with the wind blowing through her long, thick black flowing hair. She was completely free to let her hair dangle. There was no hijab to keep her in bondage. She could see herself free,

free as the wildflower blowing in the wind and reaching up with its petals toward the blazing sun for nourishment.

A jubilant smile broke out across Sakina's face. The loud screaming voices, the agony of making bricks and the intense heat of the hot oppressive sun, had melted away in her vison. Sakina felt as free as the wildflower, free from fear, free from oppression, free to be the woman that she longed to grow up and become.

Sakina opened her eyes and pried her finger up underneath the corner of her hijab that wore tightly across her forehead. She sighed in frustration.

"Why? Why must I wear this and conceal my hair and beauty?" She lamented. *" Why is it my fault if a man sins because he's seen my hair? Why do I have to hide my hair to keep him from sinning?"* Sakina shook her head in frustration. *"He has the problem, not me!"*

Sakina sighed and gazed back down at the wildflower. She gently caressed it between her fingers and stared at its innocence and beauty. She leaned back against the trunk of the tree. Her name *Sakina* had a rich meaning. According to the Quran, her name meant, *"peace and tranquility."*

Sakina shook her head in despair. She felt empty inside. There was no inner peace or tranquility in her heart.

"Sakina Paracha," Sakina mumbled out loud to herself. *"You have no peace living here!"*

In Pakistan, women are the possessions of men. They live in constant fear of being murdered if they were to bring shame or dishonor on their families. If a woman decided to marry a man of her own choice, if she tried to divorce her abusive husband or become the victim of a rape, she would be killed. Tribal customs and traditions enslaved the women of Pakistan. They had no freedom. They were owned by their families. They had no choice or voice in society.

Sakina gazed back down at the wildflower in tears. She longed to be free like the wildflower, to be different, to make choices that would bring her happiness and freedom. Her heart broke as she thought about her sister Mahtab. Mahtab had just turned 16 and in a few weeks would become the victim of a forced marriage. Akbar and Ayesha had chosen the man that she would marry. Mahtab's marriage had been arranged in order to settle a family dispute. Mahtab would become a little more than a commodity or financial arrangement to heal the feud between two warring families.

Sakina threw the wildflower down at her feet in despair. She realized in a few years she would be next! Her marriage and her life had been predetermined by her family's honor code.

"Sakina, it's time to leave! Where are you?"

The loud screaming voice of Hassan startled Sakina. She quickly stood up on her feet and emerged from behind the tree. It was her brother Hassan with her other brother Abdul, standing together a few feet away in the distance by the gravel road. They had put away their wheelbarrows for the day and were anxious to meet their father at the bus stop. Sakina raced toward her brothers. She knew they did not want to be late and miss the bus that would take them all back home to Shaheedan Wali Village. Sakina arrived at her brother's side out of breath.

"Come on! Where were you?" Hassan shouted in a confronting tone of voice.

Hassan was so much like his father, stern, controlling and compassionless. Sakina could never feel close to him. Hassan at age 14, was tall, like his father, 6ft. 1", thin with dark olive-colored skin and fluffy black hair.

"Hello Sister!" Abdul said with a gentle smile. Sakina relaxed and smiled back. She loved Abdul. He was the complete opposite of Hasan. At 16 years of age, Abdul was gentle, respectful and full of compassion.

As they left the gravel road together and climbed up the hill, they arrived on one of the main streets of the city of Mandi

Bahuddin in the central Punjab district of Pakistan. Farther down the street was a busy, dangerous intersection that was known for car accidents because traffic lights had never been installed. Cars, bicycles and horse drawn carts converged in one of the most dangerous intersections of the city.

Sweating form a hard day's work, Sakina and her brothers continued to walk along the paved roadway. Up ahead, just before the busy intersection was the bus stop. Behind the bus stop was a small courthouse with the official flag of Pakistan collapsed against the pole because there was no wind or even a slight breeze on a hot October day. Soon the temperatures would begin to plummet with the onset of winter followed by severe storms, flooding, and colder days.

Adjacent to the busy intersection was a steep hill coming down from the main district of the city. Sakina caught a glimpse of her father Akbar, emerging from the top of the hill carrying his tool box. Akbar was a contract carpenter in the city. He barely made enough to feed his family because of the deplorable economic situation in Pakistan. Struggling to stay alive, Akbar was forced to borrow money from landlords and in order to pay them back, Sakina and her brothers slaved in the hot sun almost every day at the brickmaking kiln.

Akbar was tall, towering 6 ft. 3", thin, wearing a short sleeve tan shirt and brown-colored kaki pants. His face was covered in a neatly trimmed black beard. Akbar's eyes always had a black penetrating stare that frightened Sakina. As soon as he spotted Abdul and Hassan, his face lit up with joy. He put down his tool box and threw open his arms to welcome his sons.

"Abdul. Hassan!" He shouted for joy.

Sakina stood still and stared in despair. Her father was always overjoyed to see his sons. She understood why. They were male. Males were preferred over females in Pakistan. Being born a woman felt like a curse to Sakina. There was always a celebration at the birth of a male, but mourning followed the birth of a female. The view of a woman in Pakistan was deplorable. Women were considered only useful for preparing food and giving birth to babies. The culture and tradition of Pakistan devalued the worth and dignity of a woman. A woman could not even go out alone without being accompanied by a male guardian.

"Come on Sakina, let's go!" Akbar shouted.

The compassion and excitement had gone out of her father's eyes when he gazed upon Sakina. She longed for the fatherly hugs that he gave to Abdul and Hassan. When Akbar looked at her, all Sakina could see were black penetrating eyes and a stern and controlling stare.

Sakina took a deep breath and reluctantly walked toward her father. The bus would be arriving in a few minutes.

"Fahisha!" (Urdu for, "you whore") Bhoot. (Urdu for, "you devil.")

The loud angry voices coming from a crowd of people startled Sakina.

"You whore! You devil!" The angry voices proclaimed.

A few feet away from the bus stop was a two-story red brick courthouse. Just below the concrete steps that led to the front entrance, stood a very beautiful woman wearing a purple dupatta around her shoulders.

"I have a choice to marry who I want to!" The young woman shouted back in protest.

A crowd of several men and women surrounded the young girl. Sakina noticed that each of them had something clenched in the palms of their hands. Desperate to get closer, Sakina began to lunge forward from the bus stop when the strong arms of her father prevented her.

"Stay here!" Akbar sternly commanded her.

"I should have a choice!" The young woman continued to protest. The voices became louder and more demanding.

"You must die!" One of the men in the crowd shouted.

The rest of the crowd screamed back in agreement, drawing closer to the young woman. Suddenly, two of the men in the crowd, raised their hands in the air as if they were going to throw a baseball. The young woman shrieked in horror and desperately tried to protect herself by lifting her arms in front of her face as a flurry of bricks and stones were hurled at her by the angry mob. The crowd's accusations grew extremely loud and defiant, *"Devil! Whore!"* as they drew closer to the woman, hurling stones directly at her face and defenseless body.

The woman screamed in agony as the crowd descended upon her with a barrage of stones. Suddenly she stopped screaming and collapsed lifelessly on the ground in front of the court house steps. The door to the court house flung open and two women stood at the top of the steps with their hands covering their mouths in shock. Sakina stood silently next to her father, paralyzed with fear. Her eyes widened in shock. She put her trembling hands over her mouth. Abdul bowed his head in sadness, yet Akbar and Hassan looked calmly on with little or no emotion in their eyes. They both seemed unaffected by what they had just witnessed.

The sound of screaming sirens could be heard in the distance. The crowd began to disperse. No one in the crowd had bothered to attend to the lifeless woman victim sprawled out on the ground. No one had stopped to kneel down and check for a pulse or tried to administer any life-saving first aid. The bloodied, lifeless corpse of a beautiful young woman lay crumpled at the bottom of the steps, executed by an angry crowd who had denied her right to choose her own marriage partner. She had been the victim of a senseless honor killing in broad daylight and no one dared to come to her rescue.

Sakina stared out the window of the bus and gazed intently at the sunset. She was sitting in the rear of the bus along with the other women. The men were privileged to sit up front in the first six rows of the bus while the women took their proper places in the last few rows toward the rear.

Closing her eyes, Sakina leaned her head back, struggling to relax. All she could see in her "mind's eye" was the innocent young woman desperately pleading for her life while a circle of angry men hurled bricks and stones at her face. Tears filled Sakina's eyes. She felt numb, alone and terribly afraid. She couldn't talk to anyone on the bus. Her mind was filled with the terrifying images of cold-blooded murder! Sakina had never witnessed a murder before until today. She had heard the horrifying stories of men throwing stones in the face of women for leaving their homes without permission. She had even heard of women accused of adultery, being buried in the ground up to their chests and stoned by their family and relatives.

Sakina lived in a culture where family honor was supreme and both men and women were made to conform to a system of with no freedom of choice. Wiping the tears from her eyes, Sakina turned back toward the window. Her heart began to pound faster from anxiety and stress. Sweat beads began to roll down her cheeks. She felt trapped and desperately wanted to escape. Bowing her head in tears, she could see images of the Statue of Liberty in her "mind's eye" from the pictures of her history book. Sakina longed to one day leave Pakistan and come to America where there was real freedom to realize all of her hopes and dreams. She was tired of being a prisoner of her culture where her life was planned and determined by her controlling family. All Sakina had to look forward in the next four years was more agonizing brickmaking and marriage to a man her parents had chosen, a man she didn't even love and yet she had no choice or say in the matter.

****

The bus turned the corner and descended down the hill arriving in the village of Shaheedan Wali. It was nearly 6 pm and darkness had begun to fall. Sakina followed her brothers down off of the bus. The bus had pulled up in front of their apartment building. The Paracha family lived on the second floor of an apartment building complex that was built beside a grocery store and the local post office. Akbar paid *50,000 rupees a month ($979.00)* to provide a dwelling place for his family. Being a carpenter didn't provide enough money for his monthly rent so Akbar enlisted his children's assistance to help him out. Both Abdul and Hassan had begun working at the early age of 9, almost every day from sunrise to sunset so that their family could survive. While Ayesha and Mahtab remained at home to cook, clean and keep house, Sakina joined her brothers to also earn money. The unbearable financial pressures and the deplorable economic conditions in Pakistan made life miserable for the Paracha family. There was very little rest and relaxation for Sakina. She had no time for having fun with her friends, just laboring in the hot sun, making bricks, to pay off her father's debts!

Sakina followed closely behind her brothers through the front door of her apartment. Her nostrils were immediately greeted by the delicious aroma of chicken biryani cooking on the stove. Chicken Biryani was Sakina's favorite food. The wonderful smell of garlic, onions, and chili powder on a bed of rice with cut up chicken pieces was a welcomed ,heavenly aroma after a hard day's work of making bricks.

Ayesha and Mahtab were hard at work in their tiny little kitchen setting the table for dinner as Sakina walked in the door. They had begun cooking three hours earlier when the electricity had finally come back on. The number one problem Pakistan suffered with was daily power outages. Power outages crippled Pakistan, sometimes lasting up to 22 hours a day, effecting over 180 million people. The economic cost for providing electricity cost over 10 billion dollars a year. The power outages were the source of civil unrest and rioting as protesters demanded that the government do something to fix the problem. Some families, who were wealthy enough to afford generators, were able to survive the energy crisis. However, that was not the case with the Paracha family. They had one ceiling fan that was located in the living room that provided some relief from the brutal heat. While the electricity was off, Sakina and her family laid cold, wet towels over their faces until it came back on.

Sakina's apartment on the second floor was tiny and cramped. Upon entering through the front door was the living room with a tarnished hardwood floor with two red-colored circular rugs. There was no television, only a radio on a small table by a lamp, reserved for Akbar, who loved to listen to "radio Pakistan." Akbar would come home after a hard day's work and plop himself in a recliner chair next to the table and listen to the news and Islamic lectures until he fell asleep. Akbar hated any kind of western influence or entertainment, therefore television was forbidden in the Paracha home.

Next to the recliner chair was a worn-out couch with tears and rips in the fading cloth material. Akbar had purchased it cheaply at the local junkyard. Down the hallway were three tiny bedrooms, one bathroom with a leaky toilet and a small shower. One bathroom for six people! Hassan was constantly pounding on the door to "hurry up" Sakina and Mahtab who both took too long in the shower and primping in front of the mirror.

The monthly rent was a difficult challenge for Akbar to meet. Just below their apartment lived a family with two newborns that kept them awake many nights, crying and pleading with their mother to feed them. The couple that lived below were constantly fighting. They never seemed to get along. Sakina woke up most every night to shouting voices and crying babies. The next day she was barely able to keep her eyes open to make bricks.

"Hi sister!" Mahtab shouted, rushing up to Sakina and giving her a big hug.

Mahtab was the love of Sakina's life! She was extremely close to her sister. She could tell her anything and they would spend hours in bed together each night talking about their hopes and dreams for the future. Mahtab was the same heights as Sakina, 5'10", with short brown hair and beautiful mesmerizing black eyes. She had just turned 16 and in a few days, she would be married, breaking Sakina's heart. Sakina would be lost without her sister and best friend. She would have no one to talk with anymore.

Mahtab and Sakina had laid awake for many nights, discussing the arranged marriage. Mahtab had been angry and depressed. She didn't love the man her parents had chosen for her. Sakina was very concerned about her sister. She had spent hours crying in bed desperate to escape the horrors of a forced marriage.

****

Ayesha paused from sitting the kitchen table and looked up toward Sakina with a warm smile. Ayesha was a dedicated wife and mother. She was barely 5'3" inches tall, with short black hair, mingled with some gray streaks. She pushed down her silver rimmed glasses over her nose and stared intently into Sakina's eyes.

"We are having your favorite food tonight, Sakina. Chicken Biryani."

Sakina's eyes beamed for joy. *"Thank you mother and of course, you too, dear sister!"*

******

After a delicious meal, Sakina helped her mother and sister with the dishes. They still washed and dried the dishes by hand, unable to afford the high price luxuries of having a modern dishwasher. It was now 7:30 pm. Sakina had a lot of studying to do before bed time. Tomorrow was Wednesday. She attended school twice a week and then it was right back to the brickmaking kiln.

As Sakina left the kitchen, she could hear the Islamic lecture on the radio coming to an end. Akbar reached across the table and turned off his radio and relaxed back in his recliner. Sakina quietly walked into the living room, careful not to disturb her father. He loved to listen to the radio and then fall asleep in his recliner chair.

"Father," Sakina meekly said.

Akbar slowly opened his eyes and stared intently at his daughter. Sakina was standing a foot away from the chair with a guilty looking expression on her face.

"I'm sorry to disturb you, father," Sakina said with a trembling voice.

Akbar sat up in his recliner chair and took a deep breath.

"Aren't you supposed to be doing your homework?"

Sakina bowed her head in guilt for a moment and then looked up at her father again.

"Father, I-I-I," Sakina nervously stuttered, *"I don't understand."*

"Don't understand?" Akbar inquisitively answered.

"Yes," Sakina replied, nervously swallowing. *"Why wouldn't someone help that lady today? Why did they let her die?"*

Akbar took another deep breath and leaned forward with a serious look on his face.

"I know about this woman. I know her family," Akbar shook his head in disgust. *"Sakina, your parents know what is best for you."*

Sakina began to cower in fear.

"This woman," Akbar explained in a bitter tone, *"this woman thought that she knew better. She decided to marry someone other than what her parents had chosen."*

Akbar's voice grew louder. *"Sakina. Learn this lesson well. Obey your parents and never dishonor or put them to shame. Do you understand?"*

Sakina was gripped with fear. She felt paralyzed, unable to respond. After a few moments, she composed herself and regained the courage to speak once again.

"But father. Did they have to kill her?"

Akbar leaned back in his chair in frustration and thought quietly for a few moments. Then he leaned forward again with a defiant look in his eyes.

"This woman had not only dishonored her parents and family, but also Allah," Akbar's eyes grew wide with rage. "*We must never dishonor Allah. Those who do that are worthy of death!"*

Akbar's words penetrated Sakina's heart like sharp knives. Beads of sweat rolled down her cheeks. She turned and hurried out of the room to find a place to hide.

****

Sakina stood in her bare feet, dressed in her night gown, gazing out of the bedroom window at the full moon. She was mesmerized by the ominous glow of the full moon shining brightly in the star speckled night sky.

She closed her eyes and imagined for a moment floating aimlessly in the universe away from the pain and suffering and connected to the cluster of planets and stars. For a fleeting moment she had forgotten about the woman who had been senselessly murdered by an angry mob before her eyes today.

"Aren't you coming to bed, Sakina?"

Sakina turned away from the window and looked at her sister Mahtab, comfortably tucked into bed.

"Yes, I'm coming," Sakina replied, climbing into bed next to her sister.

She lay still for a moment, staring up at the ceiling, without saying a word. Then she turned on her side facing Mahtab. Mahtab's eyes were closed. Sakina could sense that she was depressed about the upcoming arranged marriage.

"Mahtab," Sakina softly whispered.

Mahtab remained still with her eyes closed.

" Today at break time, I walked to the water fountain and discovered the most beautiful batch of wildflowers growing near a tree."

Mahtab mumbled something underneath her breath, half asleep, barely paying attention to what Sakina was saying. Sakina's face glowed with joy as she closed her eyes remembering the experience at the kiln.

"I picked up a beautiful yellow dandelion and began to pluck its petals off, Mahtab. I thought about us when I did that. I thought how wonderful it would be if we were like the wild flower."

Mahtab opened her eyes with a peculiar grin on her face. She turned her head, gazing at Sakina.

"What are you trying to say?"

Sakina had look of hope on her face. Her eyes sparkled with wonder.

"I wish we could be like that wildflower, blowing free in the wind, growing wild and free. I wish we could both be free, Mahtab. I wish we didn't have to live in fear by so many rules, so many do's and don't's and we could be free and beautifully blowing in the wind like the wildflower."

Mahtab's lips began to tremble with emotion. Tears filled her eyes. Sakina reached over and ran the tips of her fingers through her sister's soft brown hair.

" I'm sorry. I'm sorry, Mahtab. I'm only trying to help you feel better."

Mahtab shook her head in despair.

"I don't love him. I don't love him!" She moaned in protest. *"Why? Why do I have to marry Hoosein? I didn't choose him. Why?"*

Sakina turned over and laid on her back again, feeling guilty for upsetting Mahtab.

"I do feel like the wildflower," Mahtab said in anger, *"a flower that has been crushed and trampled. I feel like I'm being sold. I don't feel human. I have to marry someone to settle a family dispute."*

Mahtab's voice cracked with emotion as tears streamed down her face. Sakina laid quietly, afraid to say another word. Then she reached across and held her sister's hand. Tears streamed down her face.

One day, Mahtab, one day we will be free like the wildflower."

Chapter Two

Sakina the schoolgirl

Sakina walked beside Abdul along the gravel road which led to her school. It was 7:30 am and twice a week, Abdul would escort his sister in the early morning hours to school, which was a ¼ mile walk from their apartment dwelling. Sakina wasn't allowed to walk by herself. Every woman in Pakistan had to have a male chaperone with them when they left home. While walking into the village to go shopping every day, Sakina noticed that the women would never walk beside their husband, but instead would follow behind them in keeping with the patriarchal traditions of the culture. Submissiveness was a high duty and priority for every Pakistani woman. Sakina remembered hearing horror stories of women who were beaten or buried alive in a grave by their husbands if they broke with tradition and left home alone without permission.

The early morning air was unusually cool this morning. Soon the winter season would arrive in Pakistan and the brutal summer heat would be replaced by a cold wintry climate of storms and floods. Sakina felt safe when she was with her brother Abdul. Unlike Hassan, Abdul was kind and compassionate to Sakina. He had a gentle and respectful spirit and Sakina knew that one day her brother would become an incredible husband and father.

Sakina walked up to the front door of the red brick, one story school house, surrounded by thick, green bushes with a tall pole in the center of the courtyard, displaying the official flag of Pakistan.

"Have a good day, Sakina," Abdul said with kindness in his voice.

Sakina smiled and planted a kiss on her brother's cheek.

" Thank you dear brother. I love you!"

Walking through the front door, Sakina turned down the short hallway and walked inside of her classroom. Inside were 20 other girls, busy talking and chatting out loud to each other as they sat down at their desks. On the front wall was a large green chalkboard with a pull down map of the world. In the corner was Miss Saba's desk, filled with books and papers. Miss Saba was a young, beautiful and dedicated teacher with an energetic personality. She loved her job and was very interactive with her students. Miss Saba was also very creative, using videos and special guest lecturers to teach her students. She was committed to teaching them the basics, of history, math and classical literature to prepare them for the next level of high school once they graduated. Miss Saba also taught Islamic History and the Quran. Sakina loved history and math but struggled to become interested in Islamic history and memorizing the Quran. It was difficult for Sakina to appreciate Islamic History when she witnessed the way men treated their wives. She wondered how men could be dedicated to Allah and the Quran when they mistreated and abused their wives. *Didn't they fear the judgment of Allah?* Sakina pondered to herself. *Would Allah approve of the way they treated their wives?*

What also made it difficult for Sakina to study the Quran and Islamic history was the way her own father treated her growing up. Submission, obedience, and fear were the only three words Sakina could remember in describing her father. Her mother Ayesha lived by these three words and Sakina was determined that she wouldn't turn out like her mother and live the rest of her life being imprisoned by an abusive husband.

"Sakina?"

Sakina turned and saw Farzana running toward her from the corner of the classroom. She quickly gave Sakina a sisterly hug and kiss on the cheek. Farzana was one of Sakina's best friends. They had grown up together in the village and had been close friends for more than ten years. Farzana was wearing a yellow dupatta carefully tied around her shoulders that fit beautifully with her traditional Salwar Kameez clothing. Just below her glasses, at the side of her cheek, Farzana had a tiny black birthmark mole that Sakina used to tease her about when they were both much younger children. Ghazala, Sakina's other friend, joined them at their desk, excited to see her at school today.

"Alright class. Everyone please take their seats," Miss Saba instructed.

Sakina sat down in the first desk up front next to Farzana and Ghazala. There were a total of 20, eleven year-old girls in Sakina's class. Miss Saba pulled down the video screen.

"Yeah!" All of the girls excitedly exclaimed out loud, *"We are going to see a movie today?"*

Miss Saba smiled as she walked toward the VCR machine in the center of the classroom.

"This morning, young ladies, we are going to learn about the government of the United States....."

Suddenly there was a loud whispering coming from some students that were sitting next to the windows, interrupting Miss Saba. A few of the girls jumped out of their seats and ran toward the window to see what was happening. Sakina shrieked in terror, cupping her hands over her mouth and immediately ducking down underneath her desk. Three men with rough, black beards, dressed in jungle camouflage attire and wearing red bandanas across their foreheads, strutted into the classroom. Two of the men were carrying rifles and walking side by side next to their leader.

Miss Saba shrieked in terror, unable to move. Their leader was a tall bearded man wearing soiled tan military pants with a green belt and a red bandana across his forehead. He gazed sternly across the room at the girls with a look of fierce anger in his eyes.

*"You young girls!"*The leader sternly said, pointing his finger at them, *"You don't need to be here!"*

There was an immediate silence in the classroom. Many of the girls nervously held onto each other in fear. Sakina remained underneath her desk, bent over, holding her head in her hands and trembling with fear.

"Who are you? What do you want?" Miss Saba nervously asked.

The two other men cocked their rifles. Miss Saba began to nervously shake. The leader walked up and pressed his nose up against Miss Saba's face, staring intently into her eyes.

"Shut up! You will speak when I say you can!"

Miss Saba shook her head and swallowed nervously.

"As I said, these girls don't belong here. They should be at home! They don't need to be in school getting an education."

Miss Saba nervously shook her head, anxious to reply.

"But, but...why sir?"

Miss Saba could feel the leader's hot breath in her face.

"Education will corrupt them just like the girls in the West. Western values, western education!" The leader turned his face away and spit on the floor in disgust. *"Education is not for women! Women are the property of men! They are to stay at home and be obedient to their husbands!"*

The leader turned and gazed once again at the girls in the classroom. He could see the terror in their eyes. Then he turned and once more stared intently back at Miss Saba.

"We are the Taliban! We are here in Pakistan to institute true Sharia Law!"

During the 1970's, when the Soviet Union invaded Afghanistan, the Pakistani Army crossed the border to assist Afghans in their fight. Some of the soldiers remained in Afghanistan and became influenced by a militant Islamic fundamentalist movement known as the *Taliban founded by*

Mohammad Omar in 1994. The Taliban terrorized the Afghans in the capital of Kandahar and became well known for their brutal treatment of women. The original Taliban was composed of Pashtun tribesmen following a rigid fundamental code with a strict interpretation of Sharia Law. They terrorized and massacred many Afghan civilians believing Allah had called them to dominate Afghanistan. Since the terrorist attacks of 9/11, some Pakistani's had returned to their homeland influenced by the Taliban and were determined to convert Pakistan under a much more rigid code of Sharia Law.

The leader turned his angry face away from Miss Saba and once again stared at the young girls in the classroom. Sakina kept her head in her hands. Her whole body was shaking with fear that the Taliban would open fire on them. There was an eerie silence for a few moments. The leader gestured for his two bodyguards to follow him as he walked back out of the classroom. Once they arrived back outside, the Taliban terrorists left the school grounds quickly on foot and were immediately met by two large cargo transport trucks.

Once Miss Saba was sure that the trucks had left, she took a nervous deep breath and ran toward the children hiding underneath their desks. She hugged them tightly, relieved and thankful to be alive. The girls began to audibly moan in tears as Miss Saba held onto them tightly. Sakina rose up from underneath her desk and joined the mob of girls being hugged by Miss Saba.

*****

Abdul walked in the front door of the apartment with Sakina following close behind. Mahtab was first to greet Sakina giving her a sisterly hug.

"Welcome home Sakina, I'm so happy to see you!"

Sakina pulled away from hugging Mahtab and gave her a terrified look.

"Mahtab, you will never believe what happened today at school!"

"Sakina," Ayesha said interrupting. She had a grim look on her face. *"Your father would like to see you."*

Sakina became very quiet. Fear gripped her heart. She could sense that something was terribly wrong.

"Mother," Sakina said meekly, " *What's wrong? What have I done wrong now?"*

Ayesha's face had a look of apprehension.

"I'm not sure. Go quickly. Your father is waiting."

Mahtab stared down in despair. Sakina glanced at her sister with a desperate look in her eyes. Then she slowly and quietly walked into her room. As she walked through the bedroom door, she noticed her father sitting on her bed. She could immediately tell by the look in his eyes that he was in a horrible mood! His deep black eyes gave Sakina a fierce and penetrating stare. She was used to these kinds of situations. Akbar was under a tremendous amount of financial stress. He couldn't control his emotions and his only way of coping with his stress was to lash out at his family, especially Sakina.

"How many times have I warned you Sakina, that I would punish you severely for not getting your homework done?"

Sakina stood paralyzed with fear at the entrance to her bedroom. She could feel her heart begin to race in her chest.

"Why do you provoke me?" Akbar's voice grew louder. *"Answer me!"* He shouted.

Tears streamed down Sakina's face. Her whole body trembled.

" Why didn't you finish your homework last night?" Akbar demanded his voice raging with anger. *"Answer me!" he demanded once again.*

"Father, I-I," Sakina stuttered.

Suddenly Akbar jumped up from the bed and grabbed Sakina by her arm. Sakina recoiled and screamed in fear.

"Akbar, no!" Ayesha shouted in fear from the kitchen.

Akbar tightly squeezed Sakina by the arm. She resisted with fear and screaming, struggling to free herself from her father's grip. He threw open the sliding closet door. Sakina screamed louder in fear.

" No! No! Please father, no!"

Akbar's grip became stronger and tighter. Sakina had no strength left to resist. She fought with all of her might as Akbar pushed her up against the cold hard wall and then pulled the sliding door shut. It quickly became pitch black inside the closet. Sakina dropped to her knees in exhaustion and fear, loudly crying and moaning and terrified for her life. She began beating against the locked sliding door.

" Let me out! Please let me out!" Sakina begged in panic and fear. Then weary, afraid, and out of breath, Sakina collapsed on the dark and musty closet floor, with no energy or hope left inside of her.

*****

Mahtab looked beautiful in her elegant, red silk dress for her wedding day. The red silk dress was a gift from the Jamali family. In Pakistan weddings, a traditional dowry was exchanged between families. The Paracha and Jamali families today were burying a 20 year rift between themselves. Akbar had donated expensive jewelry to the Jamali family as a dowry payment. The arranged marriage was an agreement made between both families as a way to heal their long standing dispute.

Today Mahtab felt worthless. Even though she looked beautiful in her red silk dress with blue diamonds shaped designs embroidered into the material, inside Mahtab was miserable. She felt like nothing more than a financial arrangement and bargaining chip. Her husband Yousuf, on the other hand, was radiant with joy. He stood 6 ft. tall, stout and muscular, 225 lbs, over shadowing Mahtab, who was five inches shorting and only weighing a petite 140 lbs. Mahtab had just turned 16. Her whole world would now be focused on pleasing her husband's needs. Today she felt like a possession, a reluctant bride chained to her husband with no rights and no possibility of escape!

There had been a brief traditional wedding ceremony in the village mosque and now the wedding party had moved outside to a small park. The air was filled with the loud music of drums, flutes and guitar playing traditional India/Pakistani folk music. Several other families from the community had been busy preparing delicious lamb rogan, josh, tomato curry, meat lentil soup and Kashmiri chai tea, which was a thick creamy and sweet shake.

Mahtab struggled to smile and look happy as she mingled with the Jamali family. Sakina followed her sister as she greeted the families, accepting gifts and showing her appreciation. Ayesha walked up to her daughter and looked intently into her eyes with a reassuring smile.

"Mahtab, don't worry. You will learn to love Yousuf. He is a fine young man."

Mahtab turned her face away in shame. Tears filled her eyes.

"I don't love him, mother," she confessed, her lips trembling, as she wiped the tears from off of her cheek.

Ayehsa put her arm around Mahtab. The music became louder. People were laughing and having a great time.

"This is a very important day for our families, Mahtab. We have worked so hard, saved our money, planning for this day."

Mahtab gave her mother an angry look.

"But mother. Don't you understand? This is your day, not my day! You didn't give me a choice!"

Mahtab's voice cracked with emotion. Several of the family members heard Mahtab's outburst over the loud music and gazed toward her, giving her curious looks and stares. Mahtab bowed her head in shame. When she looked back up, her new husband Yousuf greeted her with a puzzled expression on his face.

" What is wrong with my wife? Aren't you having fun?"

Mahtab managed to crack a smile and then excused herself as she walked toward the restroom.

"She is just a little nervous," Ayesha explained to Yousuf.

Sakina watched her sister run away toward the restroom in fear and anxiety. Deep down inside she too was filled with feelings of panic and fear. In just five years she would join her sister in another arranged marriage scenario. There seemed to be no escape and no choice for Sakina. It was a dreadful feeling to be a prisoner of her culture!

Chapter Three

Sakina the reluctant bride

(Five years later)

2006 was a turbulent and catastrophic year for the people of Pakistan. It began with terrorist attacks in Lahore, killing over 100 innocent people as Sunnis and Shias fought over religious differences. Prime Minister Benazir Bhutto of the Pakistan People's Party was terrorized with death threats and during a speech was nearly killed by a crazed sniper's bullet! The year ended as the people of Pakistan prepared for the feast of sacrifice. The important Muslim holiday was tragically interrupted by a 5.0 magnitude earthquake in the mountainous district of Gul Mehra that killed over 200 families.

2006 was also the year that Sakina turned 16 and became the reluctant bride in a forced marriage to Kamal Badaui. Like her sister Mahtab, she was given no choice but became a victim to the schemes of her parents who claimed to know what was best for her life. Sakina had no choice but to submit and obey or risk offending the family honor and suffer serious consequences.

Kamal at first seemed like a sensitive and compassionate person, but once they were married, the "real" Kamal emerged into a controlling, abusive man just like her father. Kamal demanded Sakina's loyalty and attention without question. If she complained to her father about Kamal's abusive behavior, Akbar would immediately assume Sakina had done something to deserve it.

A few weeks after the tragic earthquake, Kamal and Sakina traveled to Lahore to begin the Eid-Ul-Ahza celebration, the feast of sacrifice, which followed Ramadan, one of the most important pillars of Islam. The feast of sacrifice celebrated a famous story in the Quran about the patriarch Abraham who was willing to sacrifice his son Ishmael as a test of obedience to Allah. When Allah saw that Abraham was willing to obey him without question, he provided a ram for the sacrifice, sparing his son Ishmael.

During the feast of sacrifice, Muslims all over the world sacrifice a sheep or goat and divide it into three parts. The family would retain 1/3 of the meat, giving the other third to friends and relatives and the remaining part was given to the poor.

While at the Mosque during worship, Sakina and the rest of the women were separated from the men and required to pray behind a screen so as not to distract their husbands. It was during the feast of sacrifice that Sakina reached the lowest part of her life. For most of her life she had witnessed death and violence, men abusing their wives and killing them in the name of honor. She had seen women publicly stoned, watched terrorist attacks against innocent people and listened to Muslims argue and debate about their religion.

The terror, violence and killing had emotionally drained her spiritually and caused her to question the reality of her Muslim faith. " *Why, if my religion is the one true religion,*" Sakina pondered, " *Why is there so much evil, violence and death among those who profess to be true Muslims?"*

As Sakina read the Quran, she was convinced that the problem was with professing Muslims and not its teachings. The Quran taught against murder and violence declaring,

"We ordained for the children of Israel, that if someone slew a person, unless it be in retaliation for murder, or for spreading mischief in the land, it would be as if he slew all mankind, and if anyone saved a life, it would be as if he saved the life of the whole people."

(Surah 5:32)

Deep down inside, Sakina was convinced that Islam was a peaceful religion and those Muslims that killed in the name of honor were desecrating the true teachings of the Quran. Belief in Allah was the only anchor of faith that she possessed and inspite of all of the killing and violence, Sakina desperately held on to her beliefs. Without her Faith, she would sink hopelessly deeper into darkness and despair.

The only glimmer of hope that Sakina had was the joy of being an aunt to two beautiful boys that Mahtab gave birth to. Jamal and Waheed were the absolute joy of her life. Mahtab had been blessed with two healthy boys, but unfortunately Sakina was unable to get pregnant. When Kamal saw Mahtab's children, he reacted with jealousy and rage, putting a tremendous strain on Sakina to bless him with a child.

Akbar had taken Kamal under his wing teaching him the carpentry business. He had also blessed Sakina and Kamal with a small apartment only a mile away from their home. It was a tiny dwelling with only one bedroom, a leaky toilet and a built in stove on the ground floor. Sakina was anxious to do some decorating and asked her mother to help her find some pictures of flowers to hang on the wall to add color and beauty to their tiny little apartment.

Before they were married, Kamal appeared to be a humble and compassionate man, but once he became her husband, he was transformed into a controlling and demanding ogre. He was extremely particular about how the apartment looked and insisted that Sakina spend the day cleaning and doing laundry so that when he came home from work, he could relax in his sanctuary after a hard day.

Sakina had been thrust in to a world of duty and honor, where obedience was not optional. She had been taught that as a good Muslim wife, she must always be willing to satisfy her husband sexually and could never refuse unless she was ill or having her monthly period. Being a wife was more exhausting for

Sakina than her days in the brickmaking kiln. At least as a brick maker, she could work alone and not be monitored or controlled.

This morning, Sakina had awakened early. She couldn't sleep. As soon as her feet hit the floor, she could feel a deep sorrow and heaviness in her soul. She felt despaired and troubled inside as if something horrible was about to happen!

Finishing up the laundry in the basement, Sakina climbed the stairs carrying a heavy clothes basket in her hands. She hurried into the kitchen and sat down at the dinner table, taking a long deep breath. Dinner was going to be late tonight. Sakina groaned in despair. *"Kamal will not be happy about that,"* she muttered out loud to herself.

Slowly rising up from the chair, Sakina opened the cabinet door and pulled out a skillet. Kamal loved fish and rice and pleasing him with his favorite food was her sacred duty. As she turned on the stove, Sakina heard the front door open and close. She had her back turned toward the stove as Kamal walked in and slammed his lunch bucket down on the kitchen table. He breathed an angry sigh. Sakina spun around in time to see the frustration and anger in his eyes.

"Why isn't dinner done?" Kamal demanded.

"Honey, I –I," Sakina stuttered.

Kamal rolled his eyes in frustration.

"I work hard all day and I'm hungry!" he yelled, slamming his fist down on the table.

Sakina began to tremble with fear. She couldn't remember the last time Kamal had come in a good mood and gave her hug.

"Dear, I was busy all day cleaning and doing laundry."

Kamal took another angry deep breath.

"I'm tired of your excuses, Sakina! You are not making me happy these days. I will have a talk with your father."

A single tear rolled down Sakina's cheek.

"No please don't do that!" Sakina pleaded with Kamal.

Akbar was very partial to Kamal and would always take his side in every one of their disputes. Her heart became filled with fear as she turned back toward the stove to begin frying the fish. Kamal abruptly left the kitchen after hearing two loud knocks at the front door. Sakina continued cooking at the stove. A few moments later she heard footsteps enter the kitchen once again.

"I'm hurrying as fast as I can," Sakina explained, shouting out loud thinking Kamal was angry and impatiently waiting for his dinner. When Sakina turned around from facing the stove, she was startled to see her parents standing in the doorway to the kitchen. Akbar stood in the archway, his arms folded, with an angry expression on his face. Ayesha stood next to him in tears, shaking from fear and anxiety.

"Mother! Father!' Sakina blurted out, *"What's wrong? Why are you here?"*

Kamal stood quietly next to Akbar and bowed his head, taking a deep breath. Ayesha struggled to compose herself. She slowly walked toward Sakina. Sakina began to tremble with fear.

"What's wrong? What's happened?" Sakina demanded.

Akbar took an angry deep breath and rolled his eyes, looking up toward the ceiling. Ayesha stood face to face with Sakina. Sakina had a panicked look in her eyes. She stared back at Kamal hoping for an answer. Ayesha reached toward Sakina with her trembling hands.

"It's Mahtab!"

Sakina's eyes grew wide with fear. She nervously swallowed, struggling to speak.

"Mahtab," she blurted out, *" What's wrong? What happened?"*

Ayesha gently held Sakina's hands. Sakina could see a look of desperation in her mother's eyes.

"Mahtab is dead!"

Sakina dropped the spatula out of her hands in shock. She cupped her hands over her mouth.

"Dead?" She screamed in unbelief, *"Dead? No! No! Mahtab!"* Sakina cried out in astonishment. *" Why? Why? What happened?"*

Akbar's face turned read with anger *" How could she do this to Yousef?"*

Sakina's shock suddenly melted into rage. She couldn't believe how cruel her father had become being more concerned about Yousef's feelings rather than his own daughter's death. Ayesha's hands were trembling with fear and pain as she held onto Sakina?"

"Why mother. Why?" Sakina screamed in shock.

Ayesha shook her head in despair. *"I don't know. I don't know."*

"I must go to her," Sakina insisted, breaking away from her mother's grip.

"You can't" Ayesha bluntly said with a cold expression on her face.

Sakina stopped frozen in her tracks.

"I have to see my sister!" she demanded

"You can't!" Ayesha sternly replied once again. *"She set herself on fire!"*

Sakina shrieked, trembling in tears, grabbing onto her mouth with her hands. She remembered hearing the horror stories of young Pakistani women committing suicide by *self-*

immolation or setting themselves on fire in protest of the patriarchal society.

Sakina broke down in uncontrollable loud moaning and tears. She looked intently into her father's eyes. She couldn't hold in her anger anymore.

"You killed her!" Sakina screamed, *"You killed her. You gave her no choice!"*

Pushing up against her mother, Sakina bolted out of the kitchen and ran into her bedroom, slamming the door behind her.

Sakina lay wide awake staring up at the rotating blades of the ceiling fan above her head. Kamal was asleep next to her. He had no trouble falling asleep tonight. Nothing ever bothered Kamal. He very seldom showed his emotions. Even tonight after witnessing how upset Sakina was after hearing the news of her sister's suicide, Kamal remained calm and devoid of any sympathy or emotion. Every time Sakina would close her eyes, she would see Mahtab's face in her mind's eye. She could never forget the despair and sadness in Mahtab's eyes at her wedding. For months, Mahtab suffered with depression, unhappy and devastated, that she was forced to marry a man that she didn't love.

Sakina opened up her eyes. Her heart was so heavy with grief that she felt suffocated and trapped. Unable to sleep, Sakina rose up from the bed and touched the floor with her bare feet. She bowed her head in tears once again. The grief had become too much for her and now her mind was made up.

Tiptoeing quietly out of the bedroom, Sakina walked into the kitchen. After a few moments she switched off the lights and went into the bathroom closing the door behind her. She knelt down on the cold, hardwood floor and quietly began sobbing. Her heart was filled with darkness and pain. She was overwhelmed with sorrow and sadness. Sakina's hands began to tremble with fear.

"Allah! Allah!" Sakina sobbed out loud, "Please forgive me."

She slowly reached into the pocket of her pink nightgown and pulled out a sharp shiny kitchen knife. Immediately she burst into tears, overcome with guilt. She clasped both of her trembling hands around the handle of the knife holding it directly in front of her abdomen. The pain of her sister's death had become too much for her to bear. Her life ended the day she had married Kamal. Sakina was tired of being a slave to Kamal, a prisoner with no rights and no possible way of escape, except taking her life just as Mahtab had done.

Sakina closed her eyes. She could see Mahtab's face. She smiled amidst her tears and took a deep breath. Opening her eyes for one last time, she gazed down toward the shiny sharp knife clutched in her shaking hands.

Suddenly, a blazing white light engulfed Sakina. Startled and shaken, she dropped the knife from out of her hands and fell backwards on the bathroom floor covering her eyes from the intense white light that had surrounded her life a cloud.

"Sakina. Don't be afraid," a soft, tender but authoritative voice said, coming from the blinding light.

Sakina lay flat on her back, trembling with fear, trying to cover her face.

"Don't be afraid," the voice instructed her once again.

At that moment, a peace flooded Sakina's soul. She stopped shaking and lay completely still. She dropped her hands down from her face. Her eyes began to focus and she saw a man standing above her in the blazing white light dressed in a beautiful silk robe with his hands stretched out before him.

"Sakina. Don't be afraid. I am Jesus. I am your God and I am your friend. I love you."

The words that Jesus spoke brought incredible peace and comfort to her soul. All she could do was listen. She couldn't speak. She was mesmerized by the vision before her eyes.

"I bring you peace, Sakina." Jesus said.

All of the sorrow and hurt melted away from Sakina's heart and was replaced by a calmness unlike anything she had ever experienced before.

"I am your peace. I am your friend. I will lead you. I will guide you. I will never leave or forsake you, Sakina."

Sakina lay, utterly transfixed by the words of Jesus. His words were like life and healing to her soul.

Sakina. Don't worry. One day you will completely understand. I will give you a sign. Very soon, one day, you will meet a man and he will give you your favorite flower. When he gives you the flower, n you will understand and believe who I am."

Then suddenly the blinding white light vanished and Sakina was left lying once again on the cold, hard bathroom floor. She couldn't move or speak but lay completely still, utterly transformed by the incredible vision.

Chapter four

Falsely Accused

Nabeel leaned up against the cracked concrete wall of his dark and dirty jail cell in Lahore. He had just been released from two weeks of torture and interrogation in solitary confinement. He moaned in pain, clutching his stomach. The intense pain from his internal bleeding was almost too much to endure. Nabeel had been severely punched and kicked in the stomach by his brutal interrogators as they tried to force him to recant his faith in Christ and return to Islam. Nabeel bravely endured every punch and every kick refusing to forsake Christ.

Frustrated and impatient, his interrogators returned him to his rotting jail cell promising him that they would never give up until he became a Muslim again. Now Nabeel once again was all alone in his dark and cold jail cell where he made his home with the roaches and the rats. There were no windows, just solid steel doors and bars, no access to clean water or fresh air and certainly no view to the beautiful sunshine outside.

Nabeel had been in jail for now over a year, falsely accused of burning pages of the Quran. In Pakistan, Muslims were notorious for using the *blasphemy law* in order to persecute and torture Christians. It would be life in prison for burning the pages of the Quran and death for insulting the prophet Mohammed. Christians were a hated minority in Pakistan. They were considered unclean and inferior. The government considered Christians to be western agents on behalf of the west to promote a foreign agenda and spread corruption in the Muslim society.

Christians were treated as second-class citizens, experiencing both legal and social discrimination in the job market. They were never hired as permanent workers and because of that they were denied benefits, pensions, sick leave and vacation time. If they worked in the brick kilns, Christians were subject to physical and sexual abuse. In most cases they were pressured to convert to Islam and persecuted for their faith.

Christians suffered death and violence by extremists who were constantly burning down their churches and falsely accused by the *blasphemy law.* Christian girls were targeted by gangs and raped, being sold into sex slavery and forced marriages. Once the girls were kidnapped and raped, they were forced to convert to Islam and become the brides of extremists.

Nabeel bowed his head down toward his legs in excruciating pain. He hadn't eaten in almost two days, the pain had been so severe. Rice, bread and water was Nabeel's daily diet. Sometimes Nabeel would dig cockroaches out from the bottom of the bowl, sticking to the dry and stale rice.

For Nabeel, his journey to Christ had begun over five years ago when he converted to Christianity from Islam. In Pakistan, changing one's religion resulted in death, so Nabeel had to conceal his faith from the government. Apostates were automatically subject to the death penalty under Sharia Law. Sharia Law was a strict legislative system in Islam that oppressed the population and prevented them from experiencing any religious or political freedom.

******

Nabeel sat down in the chair facing the glass panel that divided him from visitors. His whole body was weary and sore from the many beatings he had suffered during solitary confinement. He bent over and clasped his hands over his stomach in agony. The sharp pains were attacking him again. When Nabeel was first imprisoned, he weighed over 240 pounds, but now he was much thinner because of the lack of protein and good food. He now only weighed 170 pounds. His face had become wrinkled and thinner. There were dark circles underneath his brown eyes from the many nights that guards woke him up preventing him from sleeping. The interrogators loved to tantalize him with psychological games using sleep deprivation to break his spirit. When their physical techniques failed to break Nabeel, they instead resorted to psychological tactics, determined to force him to recant his faith.

Nabeel sat back up and leaned against the chair, rubbing though his thick black hair. He hadn't shaved in many days and only yesterday was he allowed his one cold shower for the week.

"Please strengthen me Lord," Nabeel whispered out loud, looking up at the ceiling.

There was a guard positioned directly behind him keeping track of his visitation time. A light flashed on from across the glass divider and a tall, thin man dressed in a brown and white suit, quickly sat down. He flung open his briefcase and pulled out some documents. It was Samuel Khan, Nabeel's court-appointed lawyer. Samuel had been hard at work demanding that the Lahore Police thoroughly investigate the false charges brought up against Nabeel. He was convinced Nabeel had been framed with the *blasphemy law* simply because he was a Christian.

Mr. Khan picked up the phone behind the glass divider at the same time that Nabeel did.

" You look horrible! Have they been beating you again?" Samuel asked with a concerned voice.

Nabeel struggled to speak, wincing in pain. He shook his head trying to hold onto the phone because of the pain.

" I've been busy putting pressure on the prison authorities to immediately have a doctor treat your internal bleeding."

Nabeel managed to smile in the midst of his agony. *" The Lord will heal me,"* he said with a confident voice.

" The social media has your picture and story plus a petition on every human rights website. You case is getting world-wide attention. I am hopeful that there will soon be a

breakthrough, Samuel said enthusiastically. Nabeel shook his head in agreement.

" They won't break me, Samuel! I refuse to let them."

Samuel looked with compassion into Nabeel's eyes. He was impressed by his courage and conviction.

"After our visit this morning, I have an appointment with the police chief. I have two eyewitnesses that are willing to name the person who framed you and invented the whole story. They saw him light some papers on fire, claiming it was the Quran, and then having several other Muslims claim that they saw you doing it!"

Nabeel took a deep breath and looked intently into Samuel's eyes.

"I have been praying for my accusers, asking Jesus to forgive them and cause them to tell the truth."

Nabeel scooted closer to the glass pane and gazed deeply into Samuel's eyes.

"Muslims do not understand the unconditional love of God. They think I'm crazy when I tell them I'm praying for them. They hate it especially when I tell them Jesus says to love your enemies. There's only one answer to radical hate Samuel and that's radical love!"

Samuel looked down at his watch and quickly closed his briefcase.

"I have to go or else I will be late for my appointment with the police chief."

Samuel stood up. Nabeel remained seated, too weary to stand up.

"I appreciate your prayers for my meeting, Nabeel," Samuel said with a confident look on his face.

Nabeel finally stood up, grabbing onto his stomach.

"I will pray for you, Samuel. God will give you the right words to speak. I know he will defend me."

*****

"Get up!"

Nabeel was awakened from a deep sleep by a loud commanding voice. Suddenly he felt two hands grab him forcibly by his shoulders, lifting him up on his bare feet from the cold hard prison floor. He barely had a chance to open his eyes as he was dragged by two husky guards to the front door. There was a loud click and the door abruptly opened. The two guards hurried Nabeel down a dimly lit corridor until they finally arrived at a side door. One of the guards held open the door as Nabeel was escorted down the dark steps that led to the prison basement.

Immediately Nabeel recognized his surroundings. He knew where he was being escorted to now, the torture chamber! Another door clicked open as they finally arrived at the bottom. Inside the room was a long cable dangling from the ceiling. Nabeel cringed with pain feeling cramps in his abdomen. One of the guards quickly clasped his hands together with steel cuffs. Another guard instructed him to raise up both hands as he locked the end of the cable and securely fastened it to the hand cuffs.

In the corner of the room, one of the guards began to turn the crank on a pulley machine. Nabeel winced in pain as he slowly began to be hoisted up from the floor with both of hands secured to the cable above his head. Shappado was an ancient and medieval form of torture where the prisoner was hoisted off the ground with both of his arms stretched above his head. The prisoner was hoisted up by a cable and then dropped, where he would dangle in midair five feet from the ground, suspended in excruciating pain until both of his shoulders became dislocated!

There was a sudden jolt. Nabeel cried out in excruciating pain, suspended four feet from the ground, dangling in midair from a cable with both arms stretched above his head.

Out of the shadows strutted the interrogator. The interrogator was a tall, heavy set, muscular man with black penetrating eyes of evil. Nabeel's arms were shaking in excruciating pain as he dangled from the cable in his bare feet, 48 inches from the floor!

"We can make this easier, Nabeel," the interrogator promised, staring up at him with his black eyes of evil. *"I can be merciful. You have a choice."*

Nabeel couldn't look his interrogator in the eyes. The pain was getting unbearable in both arms. Sweat poured down his face. His heart raced in fear.

"Become a Muslim again and you will find mercy with the courts."

Nabeel took a deep breath, clinching hi teeth in pain, his arms shaking fiercely.

"Father, Father," Nabeel stuttered*, "Forgive them. They don't know what they are doing!"*

Nabeel was quoting Jesus when he prayed for his executioners as he hung on the cross, bloody and dying. The interrogator snickered. He motioned with his head. One of the guards, right on cue, charged toward Nabeel and delivered two fierce punches to his abdomen. Nabeel screamed in agony. Another fierce blow was struck to his abdomen. Another agonizing scream from Nabeel.

There was a pause and a brief moment of silence. Nabeel moaned. He could feel his body shutting down from the intense pain. His eyes began to roll back in his head. Exhaustion and pain had overwhelmed him. His head tilted down toward his shoulders and he lost consciousness.

Chapter Five

The Miracle

Nabeel slowly opened his eyes. Everything was blurry. His body was racked with excruciating pain. The blurriness began to fade and his eyes began to slowly focus. He could see a single light bulb dangling on a chain above his head. The smell, the feel, the dim lights, Nabeel recognized that he was back once again in his prison cell, laying on his back.

The last thing he remembered before passing out was the intense pain of being punched in the abdomen while being suspended by a cable from the ceiling of the torture chamber. Then he passed out. Now he had regained consciousness and found himself on his back unable to move. His shoulders felt like they had been stretched beyond their limits. The soreness, the intense pain, the nausea....Nabeel could barely see clearly out of his eyes.

"Jesus. Jesus," he moaned.

Even moaning was painful. His head was ponding in pain. The room began to spin. He hadn't eaten in almost three days. He was dehydrated. Nabeel tried to raise his hand. It began to shake. He let it drop back down beside him.

Jesus...Jesus...please deliver me," Nabeel pleaded and moaned.

Then he closed his eyes and remembered the cards and letters he had read from thousands of Christians around the world that were praying for him. He could feel their prayers right now and as he remembered, it seemed like a gentle wave of comfort and peace splashed over him, easing the pain.

"I forgive. I forgive," Nabeel moaned with tears in his eyes, remembering how Jesus taught his disciples to love their enemies and pray for those who persecuted them. He could see himself dangling in pain from the ceiling. He could see the guard punching him in the abdomen and with every punch he counted, Nabeel prayed and forgave him. He counted it an honor to suffer for the Lord.

"For you have been given not only the privilege of trusting in Christ, but also the privilege of suffering for him."

(Philippians 1:29 NLT)

The pain intensified. His heart began to beat faster. His body felt like it was going to shut down once again.

"God you're my refuge and strength. A very present help in trouble," Nabeel muttered out loud in prayer. He loved the psalms. He loved how David both praised and lamented to the Lord in good times and in difficult times. The psalms were a great source of comfort for Nabeel.

"The Lord is my light and my salvation. Who shall I fear?"

(Psalm 27:1 NLT)

The words of scripture were nourishment and healing to his broken body. The psalms gave Nabeel courage in the face of fear. In his darkest trial, Nabeel reached out to Jesus in praise despite his pain and suffering. He began to worship and praise the Lord in the midst of his darkness and intense suffering. He felt a divine presence flood his entire being. Comfort, grace, and peace overwhelmed his whole being, washing over him like a river and numbing every fiber of his pain.

"Thank you Jesus," Nabeel rejoiced in tears.

The darkness and suffering had been swallowed up in praise. Slowly his eyelids closed and he was numb to his surroundings. He drifted off into a deep sleep of tranquility and peace, forgetting everything that he had suffered from in the last hour of his existence.

****

The faint sound of voices above his head awakened Nabeel from what seemed to be a long sleep. There was a constant, rhythmic, beeping noise in the distance. Nabeel struggled to open his eyes. It was like he was engulfed in a bright haze of lights. Everything seemed blurry and out of focus. The hypnotic beeping sound was getting louder. The voices grew louder as Nabeel forced his eyelids to finally open. Sweat rolled down his cheeks.

"Help! Help!" Nabeel shouted and moaned, *" Where am I?"*he said with panic in his voice, lifting up his aching arms.

Nabeel felt the gentle and warm touch of a human hand upon his arm.

" It's okay, Nabeel. It's okay, relax. You are in the hospital."

Nabeel slowly opened his eyes. His eyes focused on the face of his lawyer Samuel Khan. Samuel's face glowed with joy.

" You are safe now Nabeel."

Nabeel glanced down at his arms. He noticed IV lines attached to the top of his hands and many monitors stationed by his bed recording his vital signs.

*"You are a very lucky man, Nabeel,"*Samuel confidently said as he drew closer to his bedside. *" The doctors had to perform emergency surgery to stop your internal bleeding."*

Nabeel groaned from the intense pain he still felt in his abdomen.

"All I remember is lying flat on my back in my prison cell," Nabeel said in a weary voice, trying to relax."

Samuel cleared his throat and smiled, leaning closer down toward Nabeel.

"I have some great news! The police have made an arrest in your case. An elderly Muslim man confessed to framing you with a false accusation that you burned pages of the Quran."

Nabeel took a deep breath and rejoiced, closing his eyes.

"God is so good!" he said with a bright smile on his face.

"The social network campaign that was organized to pressure the government of Lahore was very successful," Samuel happily reported. *"Almost 1 million people signed your online petition and emailed the government, demanding your release. You are a very blessed man, Nabeel!"*

"Thank you! Thank you! God bless you," Nabeel softly said in a weak voice reaching toward Samuel with his trembling hand.

Samuel gently touched Nabeel's hand.

"It is my pleasure. I am also petitioning the local government to repeal the extreme aspects to the blasphemy law so that Christians cannot be falsely accused like you were."

Nabeel took a deep relaxing breath.

"You are truly an angel sent by God, Samuel."

Samuel nodded his head in gratitude and looked down intently into Nabeel's eyes.

"You need to get some rest now, Nabeel. I'm so happy to tell you all charges against you have been dropped and you are now free to return home again to your family."

Tears of joy flooded Nabeel's eyes. He closed his eyes and relaxed. God had vindicated him today and exposed the enemies that were trying to destroy his life! His prayers had been powerfully answered through the millions of faithful Christians who had been his voice when he was voiceless and spoke to the governmental powers demanding his freedom.

Nabeel went back to sleep, dreaming about the incredible home coming he was about to experience with his family.

Nine Years Later

2015

Key West, Florida

Chapter Six

Key West

Shawn Akerman walked up to the podium carrying a hot cup of coffee in one hand and a briefcase in the other. Arriving at the podium, he glanced behind to the large video screen and then pressed a key on his lap top computer. A picture of the new Cyber 6 cell phone appeared on the screen. Shawn took a final sip of his coffee and gazed down into the audience prepared to give his presentation.

Shawn Akerman was one of the top computer software designers for Global Vision Technologies. Global Vision served the local community and the world providing the finest technology for the average family to enjoy the latest in computers, cell phones and internet TV. It had been an incredible year for Shawn. He had successfully designed one of the finest cell phones, upgrading the speed from 5Gs to 6Gs on the network. Today he was unveiling to a large audience at the Seaside Hotel in Key West Island, the newest version of the Cyber cell phone.

Key West Florida was Shawn's new home after relocating from St. Louis. For the last year he had enjoyed the lifestyle of the tropical paradise and had been hard at work designing the latest cell phone for Global Vision. Key West Island was located in the Straits of Florida on the dividing line between the Atlantic Ocean and the Gulf of Mexico. It was a tropical paradise situated on the southernmost tip of the Florida Keys, just 90 miles from Cuba. The Key West Island was four miles long and one mile wide, filled with historic attractions, famous restaurants, museums, and beaches that welcomed tourists from all over the world. The Seaside Hotel was located on the world famous Duvall Street than ran north and south from the Gulf of Mexico to the Atlantic Ocean. The weather at Key West remained at a "balmy warm" and summer-like temperature of 83 degrees throughout the year.

Tourists loved to gather at Mallory Square each evening to be treated to an awesome sunset celebration featuring local musicians, food vendors and arts & crafts. Key West was also famous for the talented musician, Jimmy Buffet, who regularly entertained large audiences at his Margaritaville restaurant. Exotic palm trees, mile long beaches and incredible weather, brought thousands of tourists all over the world for swimming, volleyball, snorkeling, para sailing and jet skiing.

In just two days, the beaches would be swarming with young men and women celebrating spring break and that meant the police department would be extremely busy arresting underage drinkers bringing their booze and mischief to the beaches!

Shawn pressed another key on his computer to display the next graphic for his power point presentation. He held up a large screen purple colored cell phone for the audience to see.

"I am very excited to unveil to you today, the Cyber 6, large screen, super-fast, much improved cellphone, that I personally designed."

Everyone's eyes were focused on the video screen directly behind Shawn at the podium. Shawn turned toward the screen.

"This is the new and enhanced lithium battery."

Shawn turned back toward the podium and opened the case of the Cyber 6, pulling out the battery.

"This battery has five times the life than the previous one. One of the biggest complaints that I hear is, "I can't text and enjoy my phone, because the battery doesn't last long enough! I listened to all of your complaints and took them to the chief engineer and today I'm very excited to tell you that together we have solved your texting frustrations with a new improved lithium battery that is guaranteed to help you enjoy your phone without the hassle of recharging it every three hours!"

The audience responded with a rousing applause. Shawn happily nodded his head in agreement, satisfied that his customers were pleased with the new improvements.

"Faster network, longer battery life....." Shawn pressed another key on his lap top to display the next picture. He held up the Cyber 6 in his hand took a quick picture of the audience.

" This is the feature that I am the most excited about. The camera on the new Cyber 6 has the most superior HD picture quality of any phone on the market. With the HD improvement, I've also increased the storage space on the new phone so you can take as many pictures as you want."

Another round of applause erupted in the banquet room. The house lights came back on as Shawn concluded his presentation.

"There are customer representatives sitting at the tables against the wall that will be happy to sign you up to a new contract today. You can trade in your old phone and be reimbursed toward the purchase of the Cyber 6. Thank you, ladies and gentlemen. I'll be at the front here for another 30 minutes if you have any questions."

A line began to form in front of the tables as customers were anxious to purchase the new Cyber 6 cell phone. Shawn took a deep breath, pushed his glasses farther up on his nose and took a quick sip of coffee. He felt pleased with his presentation. At the young age of 35, Shawn was still single and preferred it that way. He wanted the freedom to dedicate all of his time to his job and be the best computer software designer in the business. Having a wife and children would be too much of a distraction for Shawn. He was determined to climb the corporate ladder and one day own and manage his own computer corporation.

Closing the lid of his lap top, Shawn looked up and watched a short, stocky, bald-headed man walk up the middle of the aisle.

"Oh no," Shawn mumbled to himself, cringing and looking for a place to quickly hide. It was his friend, David

Winslow, quickly making his way toward the podium. Shawn immediately knew what David wanted. For the past six months, David had been pestering him to come back to church. Shawn had tried his best to be respectful and polite, telling David that he would come back someday, but right now he was too busy with the new software designs. Being a Christian was important to Shawn, but in the last year, his work and career had literally consumed his life. Shawn believed God would understand the demands of his customers were important. Surely God understood that the world needed a quality cell phone, so it was more important for him to be hard at work designing it, rather than to occupy a pew on Sunday. Being a software designer was the intense passion of his life. It consumed every waking moment of his existence. Shawn didn't want anything or anyone to distract him from his accomplishments, so he had to prioritize his life. Sure, one day, he would go back to church, but right now his drive and ambition was to produce and market the finest cell phone in the world and make Global Vision a very happy corporation!

"Great presentation!" David exclaimed, reaching out to shake hands with Shawn. Shawn walked down from the platform and shook hands with David, standing on the carpeted floor.

"Thank you David," Shawn graciously replied, his eyes beaming with gratitude. *"Now, will you finally upgrade that old dinosaur phone of yours?"*

Shawn chuckled and poked David in his ribs. David rolled his eyes and laughed.

"You know I'm on a budget!"

"Oh, come on! Best friend's discount." Shawn replied, giving David a "high five."

David blushed and took a frustrating deep breath.

"You are always so persuasive!"

"It's my job to put this new Cyber 6 into the hands of every person in Key west," Shawn said with confidence, " *But you're not here to just congratulate me on a good presentation."*

David snickered and cleared his throat. His eyes grew wide with excitement.

"You have to come to church tonight with me!"

Shawn breathed a heavy sigh and looked down at his watch.

"It's been a busy day, David, I've got-."

*"Please! Please!, "*David insisted, interrupting Shawn, *" There will be a guest speaker at the church Shawn. He's a former Muslim from Pakistan and he has an awesome testimony!"*

Shawn felt trapped. He didn't want to offend his friend, but he was anxious to go home and relax and then make some final adjustments to the new software for the Cyber 6.

"I appreciate the offer, but-"

*"Shawn! Shawn,"*David pleaded, " *When will you ever just give it a break? I know how important your job is, but it's been six months since you've last been at church!"*

Shawn rolled his eyes in frustration.

"I promise one day, I'll be back-"

David dropped his head is despair. Shawn was pierced through the heart with feelings of guilt. David took a deep breath and gazed back up at Shawn.

"Shawn, this man was in prison in Pakistan. In Pakistan Christians are killed for their faith. We have it so easy here. We take our freedoms for granted everyday while Christians in the Middle East are struggling to stay alive."

Shawn rubbed his forehead. He realized that there was no way he was going to win this battle today.

"Okay. Okay, you win, but," Shawn snapped back, poking David in the chest with his finger, *" You owe me! You are going to sign a 2 year contract for the new Cyber 6."*

David chuckled and "high-fived" his best friend.

"Yeah. Yeah. Okay, you won't regret coming tonight. You have to hear this man's amazing testimony!"

****

Shawn relaxed back in the blue padded pews, four rows from the front stage of the church. It had been almost a year since he last attended. *New Horizons Worship Center,* located at the end of Duvall Street on the Atlantic Side, just a mile from Mallory Square, was a mega church with the latest technologies designed to attract every type of person from every walk of life. Relevant sermons, modern worship, and even a cafeteria for hungry worshipers, were some of the outstanding features of New Horizons.

Shawn fixed his eyes on the front stage of the large auditorium. Behind the stage was a large drum set, a row of stand-up microphones for singers and a large flat video screen that featured beautiful designs and pictures during the worship celebration. New Horizons was a high tech church with the latest in audio and video to enhance the broadcast quality of each service. Lights, cameras, drama skits and choirs, created an attractive atmosphere for Christians to experience an intense time of worship followed by preaching from the Bible.

Large crowds of people began to pack the auditorium and very quickly the pews filled up. David sat up in excitement and anticipation to see the special speaker, while Shawn leaned his head back against the pew after an exhausting day, hoping to conveniently drift off to sleep.

Before Shawn could close his eyes, the house lights suddenly dimmed and a single spot light illuminated a stool in the center of the stage. A short, stocky man stepped onto the stage and sat down on the wooden stool facing the audience. He lifted a styro foam cup to his lips and rubbed the hairs of his black beard. The audience relaxed and became still.

"It is an honor to be at your church this evening. My name is Nabeel and I'm from the troubled nation of Pakistan."

Immediately behind Nabeel, a picture dissolved onto the video screen showing the country of Pakistan on the map. Nabeel turned and looked intently at the screen, holding a tiny remote in his hand.

"Pakistan is predominately Muslim with a small minority of Christians who daily struggle to survive against intense persecution, discrimination, imprisonment and especially death , if a Muslim converts to Christianity."

Nabeel turned back and gazed intently into the audience, obscured by the darkness of the auditorium.

"Twelve years ago, after much searching, studying, and desperation, I left Islam and embraced Christ. I left an empty religion of rituals, violence and oppression and embraced a loving savior who accepted me just as I was."

Tears began to fill Nabeel's eyes. He paused and took a deep breath.

"I don't hate Muslims. Muslims are dear to my heart. I pray for my family and friends every day to find the peace, the unconditional love, and forgiveness in Christ."

There was an eerie silence in the auditorium. David nodded his head in agreement. Shawn looked down at his watch. It was 7:30 pm. All that he could think about was a cool glass of wine and relaxing in his recliner chair right now. Nabeel took a quick sip of water and cleared his throat.

"As I look around your worship center, I am impressed at the size, the state of the art production center for videotaping the sermons, the nice carpeting, the padded pews....You have a very beautiful, modern church."

Nabeel paused and pressed a button on his remote.

"Let me show you a picture of my church, or what was left of it."

A picture appeared on the video screen. Several people in the audience gasped in horror. On the screen was the remains of a church building scattered in pieces on the ground, charred pieces from an intense fire with dead bodies of Christians lying underneath the broken windows and chairs.

"This was my church in Lahore. One morning during worship, a large group of Muslim extremists broke down the doors and opened fire on Christians inside. All that I remember was crawling underneath the pews and listening to the horrible screams of my brothers and sisters being gunned down!"

Nabeel was overcome with emotion. He struggled to continue.

"I remember coughing and choking and being overcome by intense heat and smoke. After killing all of the Christians, they proceeded to torch the church building, soaking it in gasoline. It was a miracle that I escaped alive, but as soon as I was outside, I was seized by the extremists and accused of burning the Quran. They had attacked our church because some Muslims in the village told them that members of my church had burned pages of The Quran.

I spent the next two years in prison in Lahore until my good lawyer friend Samuel was able to get a confession of a Muslim in the village that had deliberately framed me because he hated Christians."

Nabeel paused and opened up his Bible. A verse from the Bible illuminated the video screen.

"I would like you to please turn to Luke Chapter Nine in your Bible and let's begin reading at verse 23. Let's listen to the convicting words of Jesus."

“Then he said to the crowd, “If any of you wants to be my follower, you must turn from your selfish ways, take up your cross daily and follow me. If you try to hang onto your life, you will lose it, but if you give up your life for my sake, you will find it.”

Nabeel turned away from gazing at the video screen and faced the audience once again. He had a serious and convicting expression on his face.

"Jesus carefully lays out to the crowd, to those that were following him because they witnessed the miracles, he lays out the requirements of becoming a follower, a disciple. First, deny yourself. Second, take up your cross daily and third, follow in obedience."

Nabeel paused and ran the tips of his fingers across his beard, deep in thought, carefully choosing the right words to say. He clicked a key on his computer. The picture of a beach party appeared on the screen. There were a few murmurs and chuckles that could be heard in the audience.

"Here at Key West, it's a virtual tropical paradise."

Nabeel thought for a moment about what he was going to say next.

"I love the beach, the warm weather, swimming, sailing, scuba diving, just like you. I love lying out in the sun, relaxing without a care in the world."

Nabeel stopped and took a deep breath.

"Unfortunately, today's Christianity is much like the picture of the beach party. No worries, no cares, no concerns, no involvement. One big party in paradise, without any pain, without any suffering..."

Nabeel paused again, shaking his head in disgust.

" Today's Christianity would be shocked at the words of Jesus! "Deny self. What do you mean Jesus?" Nabeel said in a mocking tone. *" Take up your cross? What?,"* Nabeel said with a shocked expression on his face. *" But Jesus, we didn't sign up for that! Suffering, death, persecution."*

Nabeel looked intently into the audience with a sad and frustrated expression on his face.

"We are busy partying and celebrating, uninvolved and detached from the rest of the world, while across the ocean, our brothers and sisters are rotting in prison on death row for believing in Jesus!"

There was a dead silence in the auditorium, without any murmuring or chuckling.

" The Bible admonishes us in Hebrews 13:3,"

"Remember those in prison, as if you were there yourself. Remember also those being mistreated, as if you felt their pain in your own bodies."

"We need to feel the pain and suffering of our brothers and sisters so we can faithfully connect with them in prayer.

Returning to our passage in Luke, notice in this verse that Jesus didn't say, just bow your heads, pray this prayer after me and walk down the aisle. Instead of an altar call to health, wealth and prosperity, Jesus issued a summons to commitment, the giving of our lives to follow him. Jesus makes it clear. If you want to be my disciple and follow me, you must first be committed to doing my will. You must be willing to put aside your plans and self-interests and become a living sacrifice. In other words, it is no longer my will, but your will be done, O Lord!"

Nabeel took a quick sip from his water bottle.

" Second, Jesus explains in vivid terms that those who wish to follow him must be willing, if necessary, to die. This separates the true from the false disciple. The false one hates suffering and persecution and will do anything to avoid it. Therefore, he is

easily offended at the cost of discipleship and will not be loyal to Christ.

The true disciple understands the cost of following Jesus and will remain faithful even if it costs him his own life."

Nabeel clicked a key on his computer. A picture of Christians in prison came up on the video screen.

"In Pakistan, the interrogators spend long hours beating and torturing Christians, determined to break their spirit and cause them to deny their faith and return to Islam."

Nabeel rolled up his shirt sleeve, exposing the scars on both of his arms.

"My interrogators burned my arms with hot pieces of steel. I will never forget the intense pain that I felt! I screamed in agony!"

Nabeel paused. Tears welled up in his eyes.

"I prayed to Jesus for strength, and in that moment, I remembered clearly the words, "You must take up your cross daily and follow me."

Nabeel took a deep breath, struggling to find the right words to say in conclusion.

"Tonight, if there are some of you here that have strayed away, have become hard of heart and you feel that you have sinned and failed God, I urge you, please come back. God is forgiving. God is merciful. He welcomes you back like the father who hugged and kissed his wayward prodigal son. Tonight, recommit your life to Jesus, if you have strayed. Jesus has the very words of eternal life that you cannot find anywhere else."

Nabeel laid down his Bible on the wooden stool and looked passionately into the faces in the audience.

"I love the church. It's the church Christ died for. He is the Lord and the head. He is calling us to be faithful followers, to understand the real cost of following him. It's time to awake from

our slumber and sleep and recommit our lives to him. Jesus is my treasure. He is more precious to me than anything that this world can offer. Please come back to him and let him be your first love again tonight."

The church congregation stood to their feet giving Nabeel a standing ovation, impressed by his incredible testimony. Shawn breathed a sigh of relief. It was finally over. He quickly said his good byes to David and excused himself. He couldn't wait to get home to his condo on the beach and kick back with a cool refreshing glass of wine to end the day.

Chapter Seven

The Death Blow

The Global Vision seaside office in Key West was a very busy operational center. Shawn was exhausted from making preparations for two more critical speaking engagements to display the new Cyber 6 phone in Atlanta and Los Angeles.

Friday had finally arrived and Shawn couldn't wait for some serious rest and relaxation on the beach before flying out to Atlanta. Key West had been transformed into a bee hive of tourist activity with the arrival of the spring break crowd. Thousands of teenagers and young adults had converged onto the tropical paradise with their appetite for booze and cruising chicks. The police department was now on high alert for the next two weeks fully expecting to break up many alcohol related brawls and arresting many under age violators for drinking.

Shawn logged off his computer and leaned back at his desk. He glanced down at his watch, just 15 more minutes before his much needed night on the beach for some well-deserved rest. Closing his eyes, Shawn began to visualize the foaming waves kissing the bottom of his bare feet.

Suddenly his cell phone rang. It was Brian Andrews, the district manager for Global Vision. He had made a surprise visit to the facility and Shawn was convinced that a long overdue raise might be coming his way.

"Yes sir. I will be right there."

Shawn turned off his cell phone and moaned in frustration. Why so late in the day? What was on Mr. Andrew's mind? Shawn reluctantly got up from his comfortable chair and straightened his black tie. The thought of a salary increase motivated him to quickly walk down the hallway and catch the elevator. In just 15 minutes, Shawn entertained the delightful possibility of waltzing out of Mr. Andrew's office with a raise and two days of pure fun on the beach.

Brian Andrews stood up from behind his desk. He was tall, 6ft, 1" with sandy blonde hair, dressed in a sharp two-piece, black pin-striped suit and yellow tie.

"Please sit down, Shawn," Brian respectfully said, pointing to the chair.

Shawn extended his hand. Brian warmly shook it. They both sat down across from each other and relaxed.

"I'm sorry. I know it's late and you're anxious to enjoy the weekend," Brian said.

"No problem, sir."

Brian looked down at his desk and nervously tapped the pen in his right hand. He had a serious expression on his face. After a few moments he folded his hands and looked up intently into Shawn's eyes. Shawn nervously smiled back, anxious to hear the good news.

"Shawn," Brian began, clearing his throat, *"You are one of Global Vision's finest computer software designers."*

Shawn's heart began to race with excitement. He tried to compose himself and pretend as if he didn't know what was coming.

"You did a great job on the new design of the Cyber 6."

Beads of sweat began to roll down Shawn's cheeks. He braced himself for what he was sure would be good news for all of his accomplishments. Brian looked down at his folded hands and took a deep breath.

"Even though Shawn, we are very pleased with your hard work, as you know, our stocks have been down for the last month."

Shawn shifted nervously in his chair. Sure, he had heard about that, but was confident they would go up soon with the release of the Cyber 6.

"The "higher ups" have been frustrated with the lack of pre-orders for the new phone."

Shawn anxiously bit his lip. What? He had never heard anything about that. This was a complete shock! Brian took another deep breath.

"Management is concerned that our overseas offices and our nationwide offices may be losing too much money. Stocks are down, sales are down."

Shawn wiped the sweat from off of his forehead.

"What are you trying to say, Mr. Andrews?" Shawn nervously asked.

A look of frustration came over Brian's face. He leaned closer to Shawn from across his desk.

"Management is immediately doing a restructure of the departments to boost the sales of the cell phones and internet, which means..."

Shawn swallowed nervously and shifted in his seat.

"Which means Shawn, I have to begin here in Key West. I'm very sorry but I have to terminate your position immediately."

It felt as if someone had landed a solid lethal blow with their fist to Shawn's abdomen. Shawn struggled to catch his breath, His heart seemed to leap out of his chest. For a full minute he was utterly speechless and unaware of his surroundings. His dream of a new raise and a weekend at the beach had just been shattered by the death blow of his life!

Shawn stood in his bare feet on the hot stinging sands of South Beach with a large chair strapped across his shoulder. The bright rays of the early morning sun shined down on the waves of the Atlantic Ocean, glistening and reflecting like a millions sparkling diamonds. The beach was already swarming with hundreds of young students ready to have the paradise party of their life during spring break. The tall palm trees swayed in the gusty wind just a few feet from an intense volleyball match. In the distance, near the horizon, a flock of seagulls dove down upon the ocean in search of fresh fish for their early morning breakfast, while a convoy of jet skiers crashed through the choppy waves at high speeds. The beach was alive with the early morning adventurers, escaping the stress of life and connecting with the mystical call of the deep blue ocean.

Shawn took a deep breath and filled his lungs with the refreshing seaside air. The beach was his escape, his refuge, his hiding place, from the most devastating news of his life. Just last week, his world had been shattered. The love of his life had been cruelly taken away from him. Yet Shawn refused to engage in asking "why" or spending the rest of his life absorbed in self-pity. Yes the news sucked and yes life had suddenly turned cruel and unfair, but Shawn had made up his mind last night that he would not be defeated.

The sound of hip hop music with creative lyrics and pounding drum beats filled the air and set the mood for adventurous teenagers battling it out in an intense volleyball match. It was already a balmy and humid 86 degrees at 9:30 am. The sign in front of Shawn, nailed to the trunk of palm tree announced:

"Welcome to South Beach, Key West, Florida.

Southernmost beach in the continental USA

Beach chairs $5.00

Beach rules: no glass or coolers.

No dogs, alcohol or moonshine on the beach by city ordinance.

Shawn laughed out loud and pushed the sunglasses back up over his nose. Hidden in his beach towel were three plastic bottles filled with Jack Daniels and coke. Today he planned to plop his but in a recliner chair underneath a palm tree and umbrella and get horribly drunk! Alcohol had been a nasty habit in the past for Shawn, that is, until he was promoted to Computer software designer at Global Vision.

However that had all changed a week ago. Jack Daniel and coke had once again become his best friend. His best friend had a marvelous calming and numbing effect that helped him forget all of the chaos and misery in his life. Today at the beach he had a very special date with his best friend and very soon all of his troubles would disappear under the umbrella.

Shawn opened up his blue umbrella and stuck the pointed end down deep in the sand overtop of his recliner chair. He watched the little children stick their bare feet into the waves splashing against the shoreline and then run away laughing.

Shawn took a deep breath inhaling the wonderful aroma of the sea breeze blowing against his face.

"Amen! I'm home!" He exclaimed with a chuckle then fell back into his recliner chair facing the happy crowd of beach-goers playing in the rolling waves crashing onto the shoreline. Shawn laid his head back and relaxed, mesmerized by the hypnotic sound of the waves kissing the shoreline and the screams of laughter from the happy beach-goers. He was determined not to dwell on being terminated, but instead absorb every minute at the beach and fill his eyes and ears with the sounds of paradise.

Shawn could feel the hot rays of the sun beaming down on his bare legs. Within a few hours he would be as red as a lobster, but he didn't care. Paradise was calling him. That was all that mattered. He reached down into his knapsack and pulled out one of the plastic bottle. Gazing over at the volleyball game, he looked intently at the beautiful blonde women scantily dressed in their tiny green bikinis. It was a wonderful sight to behold.

"Here's to you!" Shawn exclaimed, holding up his plastic bottle of Jack Daniels to toast the beautiful women volleyball players.

Then he gulped down his "best friend" like it was his last drink. He quickly finished his first bottle and quickly pulled out another one. He held it up to his face.

"You are the best friend that anyone could ask for."

Shawn held up the plastic bottle toward the blazing sun. *"Cheers to Mr. Sun,"* he laughed and guzzled it down.

******

It seemed like Shawn had lost track of the time. He suddenly sat up in his recliner chair, gasping for breath and then hiccupping.

"Haaaaaa," he laughed out loud. The beach seemed to be spinning. His head felt extremely tight. Every move that he made suddenly felt like slow motion. Shawn realized that he was very drunk! Something whizzed past his face and nearly knocked him out of his chair. It was the volleyball.

Shawn tried to stand up but couldn't maintain his balance and immediately fell across his recliner chair. The volleyball players erupted into laughter as Shawn struggled to stand up in order to retrieve their ball. Finally he managed to stand up on his feet but was weaving from side to side. He received a standing ovation from the players. Taking a delicate few steps, Shawn finally picked up their volleyball and then stumbled forward.

"Here you go!" he yelled and then as he tossed back their ball, he tripped and fell forward face down on the hot sand. Immediately there was laughter and another round of applause.

Shawn was humiliated. He lay completely still and face down in the sand.

"May I help you?" a voice asked.

Then Shawn felt a hand pulling him up from being face down in the sand. He sat up, spitting out the grains of sand from inside of his mouth. He then began brushing out the sand from his hair. Shawn looked up. His vision was blurry and his head couldn't stop spinning.

"Are you okay?" the voice asked.

Finally Shawn was able to focus his eyes once again. He saw a short, stocky man with olive colored skin and a short black beard, stooping down over him and holding out his hand.

"You must be Shawn. I'm Nabeel. Do you remember us meeting last weekend?"

Shawn weaved back and forth from his sitting position in the sand. He could barely keep his balance sitting. Nabeel observed that he was very intoxicated. Shawn finally composed himself and looked directly at Nabeel with a glassy-eyed stare and chuckled.

"Oh yeah! You're the preacher man David took me to see!"

Shawn rolled his eyes and then gave Nabeel a puzzled look.

" How did you find me, preacher?"

Nabeel sat down next to Shawn in the sand and looked intently into his eyes

"David has been trying to call your cell phone for days. He got worried so he called your work and they informed him that you didn't work there anymore."

Shawn snickered and then took a deep breath.

"Yeah preacher, sometimes life can be cruel."

"I'm sorry Shawn," Nabeel replied, placing his hand on his shoulder.

"Well preacher-."

"*Nabeel.*" Nabeel interrupted. "*Please call me Nabeel.*"

Shawn nodded his head.

"*Sure Nabeel.*"

Shawn suddenly became serious. He picked up a pile of sand in his left hand and squeezed it, letting it drain slowly out of the palm of his hand.

"*Like you said in your sermon, Christians suffer for their faith in Pakistan.*"

Shawn shook his head in frustration.

"*So I guess my suffering really is nothing compared to theirs.*"

Shawn rubbed the sand from out of his hands. He had a guilty look on his face.

"*I don't think the good Lord is very happy with me right now.*"

Shawn took a deep breath and looked up to the sky in frustration.

"I *haven't been to church in a very long time, Nabeel. I guess I've been too busy, so-.*"

Shawn bowed his head in despair.

"*I kind of doubt that the Lord loves me anymore.*"

Nabeel put his arm around Shawn. He could see the extreme guilt radiating from his eyes.

"*That is not true Shawn,*" Nabeel reassured him, "*The Bible teaches that God loves us with an everlasting love. He never stops loving us even when we stray away and neglect him.*"

Shawn bowed his head in his hands and began to weep.

"*I know I've failed him,*" he bitterly admitted.

"*We all fail him, Shawn, but God calls us back to him and is merciful. He is faithful to forgive us. Just like the father who saw his prodigal son one day in the distance. The Bible says that he ran to him and threw his arms of love around him and forgave him.*"

"*I don't know what I'm going to do now, Nabeel. My whole life is shattered! I loved my work!*" Shawn exclaimed, bitterly weeping.

"Shawn. This may be a blessing in disguise. God may have taken this job away because he has great plans for your life!

Shawn slammed his fist down on his leg.

"A blessing!" He shouted in anger.

"*Yes,*" Nabeel answered," *God works everything out for those who love him. Those who are called according to his purpose."*

Shawn had a dazed look on his face. He shook his head in disgust.

"*I'm sorry Nabeel. I just don't see that."*

Nabeel could feel Shawn's anguish and despair. He wanted to respect his space and give him room to breathe. He pulled out a card from his shirt pocket and handed it to him.

"*Here is my cell phone number. Please call me anytime. I'm here to listen, my friend."*

Shawn took the card from Nabeel's hand and put it in his shirt pocket.

"I appreciate you listening. I'm sorry if I don't see everything your way."

Nabeel stood up.

"That's okay. Call me if you need to talk. I'll be praying for you Shawn. God bless you."

As Nabeel walked away, Shawn pulled the card back out of his pocket and stared at it. Then he put it back in, wondering what blessing could possibly come out of the pit of hell he had found himself in.

Chapter Eight

A Murder in Key West

Detective Williams stopped down and leaned over the semi-nude corpse of a woman lying on the beach. The dead woman's gray, blood spattered tank top had been purposely pulled up over her face and wrapped around her neck, exposing her breasts.

Putting on a pair of latex gloves, Detective Williams slowly pulled the tank top back down over the woman's bare belly. Recoiling in horror, Detective Williams gasped and stood up on his feet, momentarily looking away. The woman's throat had been slashed and her face had been disfigured and grossly burned from what appeared to be acid.

"Oh my God!" Detective Ronson exclaimed, peering down at the dead woman's face.

Detective Bill Ronson had been Ron Williams's partner for the last year in the Homicide Division. They both had a good working relationship together and had successfully solved important homicide cases, making Key West a much safer resort paradise to live in.

A Photographer knelt down closer to the dead woman and took a few close-ups of her throat and face. Two tall floodlights had been erected around the crime scene. The body of the woman had been discovered about an hour ago by a young couple walking in the late hours of the secluded cove of South Beach. The cove had a reputation of attracting young lovers who wanted to avoid the late night crowds at the beach in order to be alone for some intimate love and romance.

The vibrant waves of the Atlantic Ocean crashed up against the rock formations of a tall cliff that gave the cove a gothic and mystical appeal. Detective Williams began typing some notes on his tablet. Ron Williams was a ten-year veteran of the homicide Division of Key West. Luckily the crime rate in Key West was relatively quite low. Underage drinking, bar brawls, and family disputes kept the police busy, but rarely did the homicide division have to be called in....except for tonight!

Ron Williams shook his head and breathed a frustrated sigh. Bill could see a puzzled look on his face.

"*Do you see any evidence of rape?*" Bill asked.

Ron stopped typing on his tablet.

"*The coroner will tell us for sure. I'm inclined to believe she was.*"

Ron put away his tablet.

"*Bill, Can you bring the young couple over. I want to ask them a few questions.*"

They both stepped away from the dead woman as EMT's arrived on scene to process the body. Bill returned with the young couple who had discovered the dead woman's body. The young girl was very distraught holding onto her boyfriend in his arms.

"*I'm Detective Williams and this is my partner, Detective Bill Ronson. I understand you are both very upset. I just want to ask you a few questions.*"

The young man nodded his head in agreement.

"*What time was it when you discovered the body?*"

The young girl composed herself and then wiped the tears from her eyes.

"It was around 2:30 am. I-I-" she nervously stuttered.

"We were walking past the cliff, up the hill away from the shoreline, when I saw a shape of someone lying still. I figured that it was someone who had just fell asleep from being drunk. But as we walked past, I noticed the tank top pulled up over her head and then..."

The young woman paused, visibly upset and nervously swallowing.

"Did you see anyone or hear anything?" Detective Williams asked.

"No. It was very quiet except for the sound of the waves crashing gently on the shoreline."

"Before you came upon the body, did you see or hear anything unusual?"

The young girl shook her head and then began sobbing once again overcome with anxiety.

" No sir. It was very quiet. If it hadn't been for the tank top pulled up over her head, we would have kept walking, thinking the person was either drunk or asleep."

" Thank you both very much. May I contact you if I need any more information?"

"Yes of course," The young man assured Detective Williams as he began walking away comforting his girlfriend.

Detective Williams typed a few more notes in his tablet and breathed a frustrating sigh. He knew that this was going to be a very tough case to solve.

****

Shawn removed his reading glasses, leaned back in his chair, and rubbed his weary eyes. He had just spent the last two hours creating an online resume and was exhausted. Reaching across the table from his lap top, he took a refreshing sip of his favorite drink, Jack Daniels and coke.

"*Ahhhh"*Shawn moaned with satisfaction, "*You're a great friend!*" he chuckled, holding the glass in his right hand."

He sat the glass back down and returned to his computer, clicking on Google, searching for a hobby to keep him busy. Shawn was feeling anxious and frustrated. It had only been a week since he lost his job, but already he was anxious to get back to work in his software dream world. Computer programming was in his blood. His whole world had been shattered and he was determined not to engage in self-pity, but to find another software designing job as soon as possible.

He clicked on the website of Senator Ted Cruz from Texas who had just announced that he was running for president in 2016. Shawn picked up his glass and toasted the computer screen.

"*You're the man*!" He exclaimed.

Shawn was a dedicated conservative, a true patriot and a firm believer in working hard to achieve one's dreams. He hated liberalism and the philosophy that the government had to pave one's way for success from the cradle to the grave. Shawn believed in rugged individualism and hated those who sat around expecting hand outs and free stuff from the government. He believed too much government meant more taxes and less individual freedoms. The conservative view point was the only view point that worked to limit government and empower the individual to achieve his or her dreams without depending on the political leeches in Washington!

"*Should I run for office?*" Shawn laughed out loud, taking another gulp of Jack Daniels. "*Or how about the National Guard?*" He mumbled to himself.

Shawn shook his head in disgust. He was a true patriot. He was sick of how President Obama was treating the military, pulling them out of Iraq and leaving a huge vacuum to be filled by the terrorist Islamic State ISIS, who were now busy slaughtering and beheading Assyrian Christians and raping innocent young girls. Shawn slammed his glass down on the table as she glanced at a picture of Hillary Clinton.

"*Never!*" He shouted, "*You will never become president! You murdered Chris Stevens and the brave Navy seals in Benghazi,*" Shawn yelled at the computer screen in anger.

As he continued to surf the web, Shawn suddenly came upon "*Blog Talk Radio*" website. *"Create your own online radio program," he mumbled out loud in interest.*

"Hmmm," Shawn said, smiling, " *That's me!"*

Shawn knew instantly he had found a very useful hobby to occupy his time until he was back to work again. Doing radio had always interested him. Perfect! He would create an account with blog talk radio and host his own radio program on the internet.

"Wow! This is perfect!" Shawn enthusiastically shouted.

Shawn leaned back in his chair and thought for a minute.

" *What kind of program? What would I call it?"*

He thought carefully for a moment. Then he excitedly leaned forward in his chair.

"Yes. A conservative political talk program. I know, I will call it, *"Freedom lover."*

Shawn clapped his hands together in excitement and laughed. This would be the perfect hobby. He would go up to *You Tube* and find some good sound bites and edit them. Then he would create a catchy musical open and who knows, "*I could have a brand new career!"*

Shawn laughed out loud and grabbed a glass of Jack Daniel once again.

"I toast to the new, hot conservative host of "Freedom lover," a program dedicated to the destruction of Liberalism and instead the promotion of life, liberty, and the pursuit of happiness."

Shawn took a quick gulp and groaned out loud in satisfaction. He had discovered a new career today. God had been good to him!

****

Logging onto his computer, Shawn stretched and yawned. Today was a very exciting day. The debut of his radio program, "*Freedom lover.*" Shawn clicked onto the blog talk studio. A screen opened up for him to navigate for his radio program. On the right side of the screen was a list of his *mp3 sound bites* that he would play throughout his show. The first sound bite was his intro music, the loud and thundering guitars of *Stryper*, playing the *Battle hymn of the republic,* a perfect theme song. On the left side of the screen was the *guest call-in* number and spaces below for those who wanted to call in for a question or comment. In the center of the studio screen were links to promote his radio program to the social network. Shawn was ready! He called into the blog talk number and locked himself into the studio. He put on his headset.

"Three minutes until show time," the automated voice announced.

Shawn took a quick drink of hot coffee. Today he wanted to be sober and make a coherent case for the conservative viewpoint.

"One minute until show time."

Shawn quickly looked over his stories, *ISIS kidnaps 100 Yazidi women....Obama is anxious for a nuclear deal with Iran....Hillary Clinton accepts donations from countries that oppress women....police in Key West still have no clues in a recent homicide."*

Shawn took a deep breath and relaxed. He could feel the adrenalin rushing through his body.

" Ten seconds until show time."

Shawn waited patiently and right on time, the ominous opening sounds of Stryper's battle hymn of the republic began playing. He could feel his heart began to excitedly race. The thundering guitars faded from the intro. He quickly clicked on the icon to open up his microphone.

"Good morning Key West. Welcome to the debut of my new program, "Freedom Lover." A program exposing the lies of liberalism and liberating you to live your life to the fullest without the leeches in Washington, who want to chain you to the government from the cradle to the grave and slowly take away your freedoms. I'm your host, Shawn Ackerman. Welcome! Good morning internet world!"

Shawn quickly clicked on the first sound bite, a personal endorsement by Ted Cruz for president. He took a quick sip of coffee and relaxed. This morning he was feeling great! The energy and adrenalin was rushing through his body. The *Ted Cruz* spot abruptly ended. Shawn quickly switched the microphone back on.

"Ted Cruz is my man. Unlike Obama, who constantly apologizes for our country and puts more political correctness and regulations on our military, Ted Cruz is a true patriot. He loves his country. He is tough on terrorism and has the guts and knowledge to make our nation great again, empowering our military, cutting taxes, and leading the fight to once and for all repeal "Obamacare!"

1-347-857-2620, is the number to call if you have a question or comment. I want to hear from you, conservative or liberal, you are my guest. Your opinion counts on "Freedom Lover."

Shawn played a sound bite for a story about ISIS, kidnapping 100 Yazidi women and children in Iraq. He took a deep breath and chuckled.

"*Not bad for the first program,*" he blurted out encouraging himself.

The ISIS story came to an end. He turned the microphone back on and began reading the local story about a gruesome Key West homicide.

"Key West Police are still baffled by the gruesome murder of 28 year-old, Stephanie Rhine, whose body was discovered in the cove of South Beach late Saturday night. Ms. Rhine's face was disfigured and burned by an apparent acid attack and her throat had been slit.

Homicide Lead Investigator, Detective Ron Williams, says that, "At this time they have no suspects, but are hard at work pursuing leads. If anyone has any info, they are asked to call the Key West Homicide Division."

"Hmmm," Shawn muttered out loud with a puzzled look on his face. *"Key West is a very busy tourist attraction. Something like this can be bad for business."*

Shawn paused, "*Acid attack. That happens a lot in Middle Eastern countries, but is kind of rare here!"*

He put down the paper copy of the story.

"Wow. What kind of beast could do something like that to a woman?" Shawn exclaimed in a frustrated tone of voice.

As he finished his question, a phone number appeared on the left column of his studio screen. His first phone call! Shawn excitedly clicked on the number, using his mouse and connected to the caller in the studio.

"Good morning. You are live on "Freedom Lover." I'm Shawn Ackerman. What is your question or comment?"

"Good Morning," the voice replied in a middle-eastern accent, *"My name is Sakina. I'm from Pakistan. Thank you for taking my call."*

"You're calling all the way from Pakistan?" Shawn asked in an excited voice.

"No sir."

"Shawn. Please call me Shawn."

"Shawn, sir." Sakina nervously replied.

"You're English is pretty good."

Sakina nervously cleared her throat, chuckling.

"Thank you, sir. I mean Shawn. Actually I live here in Key West."

"How long have you lived here?"

"I've been an American citizen for two years. My husband and I moved here in 2013. He just graduated from dental School and opened his own business here in Key West."

"Oh, wonderful. So you and your husband live here in our little tropical paradise!"

"Yes."

"I'm sorry. Please go ahead with your question or comment."

"I'm calling in reference to your story about the acid attack victim. I just wanted to say how horrible this is but in Pakistan where I lived, these acid attacks are very common. I wanted your listeners to know that women in Pakistan are oppressed; they are second-class citizens who must obey everything that their husbands tell them to do. Pakistan is a

culture of honor and shame. In this culture, if a woman tries to marry anyone other than who her parents have chosen for her, she can be stoned because she has dishonored them. If she tries to choose her own career, she will also suffer the consequences. Women have no freedom in Pakistan."

"So you're saying Sakina that women in Pakistan must obey everything that their husbands tell them or else be killed? Are there no laws to protect them?"

Sakina thought silently for a moment.

" I believe the man who done this murder here was Middle Eastern. Cutting her throat would have been sufficient, but instead he threw acid in her face. I believe he hates women and may be targeting others. This is very frightening!"

"You should contact the police and help them solve this!"

"Shawn. I would like to invite you and your listeners to my lecture on women in Pakistan. I am a Muslim woman, but feel the need to break the silence and confront the radical Muslims who are oppressing women in acid attacks, honor killings, and forced marriages."

"You are very courageous, Sakina!"

"Thank you sir. This Friday afternoon at Florida Keys Community College, I'm having a lecture at 11:15 am and showing the film, "Prisoner of her culture." This film is a powerful documentary featuring other Muslim women speaking out for the first time in defense of their own gender and crying out for laws and reforms in Muslim countries."

"I admire you Sakina for breaking the silence."

"Well, but it comes at a cost. The Muslim community here has shunned me saying I'm giving Islam a bad reputation. I have also received death threats."

"Thank you Sakina. I will definitely come to your lecture this Friday and be educated."

Shawn clicked off the phone call.

"I urge all of you "Freedom lover" listeners to come out to Sakina's lecture and support her. She is a very brave Muslim lady!"

Chapter Nine

Meeting Sakina

Shawn opened the door to Classroom 219 at Florida Keys Community College. He glanced down at his watch. It was 11:10 am. He had finally arrived after spending all morning getting ready. The night before he had stayed up late with his best friend, Jack Daniels, in an all-night drink fest. He still felt groggy and disoriented even after a cold shower, but was determined to attend Sakina's lecture.

The room was quickly filling up with young students. Shawn gazed around the room and noticed a tall, slender young girl standing close to a video screen at the front of the classroom. She was busy chatting with an older woman. Shawn sat down toward the back of the classroom next to a young man who was busy eating his breakfast, consisting of a chocolate doughnut and a cup of coffee.

"*My name is Aaron,*" the young man quickly swallowed the last bite of his doughnut, holding out his hand, introducing himself.

"Shawn Ackerman," Shawn replied, shaking his hand with a warm smile.

Aaron gulped down the rest of his coffee.

"You a student here?"

"*No. No. I'm just here to attend the lecture.*"

"Cool!" Aaron said, nodding his head. *"I'm a student here and found the topic of honor killings very interesting, so I decided to attend."*

Shawn nodded his head in agreement and looked toward the front of the classroom again. His eyes widened with amazement as he caught his first real glimpse of Sakina.

"Wow!" he muttered quietly to himself, *"Beautiful!"*

Sakina stood nearly 6 ft. tall with long flowing black hair, olive-colored skin, beautifully tainted with make-up and heavy eye shadow. She had gorgeous, penetrating blue eyes and looked stunningly dressed in a silk pink blouse and blue jeans. Shawn was awestruck by Sakina's beauty and was puzzled that as a Muslim woman she was not wearing the traditional hijab, but instead allowed her black flowing hair to drape across her body.

The class became quiet and attentive as the time of the lecture arrived.

"I want to thank all of you for taking time out of your busy life to attend my lecture. My name is Sakina and I'm originally from Pakistan."

As Sakina finished her brief introduction, she gazed toward the back of the classroom and stopped speaking. Her eyes fastened upon Shawn. It was as if she already knew who he was before being introduced. Immediately Shawn felt a mystical connection at the moment that their eyes met. Sakina turned back looking intently at the class and resumed her lecture.

"As I mentioned before, I am from Pakistan. My husband Kamal and I came here two years ago and settled here in this beautiful resort island. Kamal began his dentist practice just last year and is making a good income. We are both so happy to live in freedom here in the United States."

Sakina reached down and pressed a key on her lap top. The scene of a violent riot in the city of Baltimore between blacks and police officers dissolved onto the video screen.

"All of us will never forget the violent images of racial rioting we saw every night in the news about the conflict in Baltimore. The protesters chanted a phrase that is very relevant to my lecture. They chanted, "Black lives matter," which is certainly true. In response, the police texted, posted and chanted back, "Blue lives matter," and of course I agree.

Sakina paused, collecting her thoughts.

" Let me say it this way. "Black lives matter. Blue lives matter and Women's lives matter!"

Sakina pressed another key on her lap top. A graphic image of a woman's body lying in the streets of Pakistan came up on the video screen. Many of the women students shrieked and moaned, reacting to the image.

" Women's lives matter," Sakina said soberly and then paused. *" This is the dead body of Farzana Parveen, a 27 year-old young woman living in Pakistan. Just a few minutes before this picture was taken, her family had hurled bricks and rocks at her in a daylight stoning. This is a common event in Pakistan. More than 1,000 women are murdered in honor killings every year. 83% of the people of Pakistan agree that a woman should be stoned! Why? What was Farzana's crime? Only this, she disobeyed her parents' wishes and married a man of her own choice.*

In Pakistan, this is called the crime of dishonor and shame. Women in Pakistan are not allowed the freedom of choice. They are shackled to their families' demands and choices. They are not allowed to choose their careers or future mates. To go against the family demands, is to bring dishonor and shame and a certain death!"

Sakina paused. Tears welled up in her eyes.

"I remember as a young child of 11 years old, when I witnessed my first public stoning."

Sakina took a nervous deep breath and wiped the tears from her face.

"I can still see the face of that beautiful young woman, crying and pleading for mercy, but received none!"

Sakina pressed a key on her lap top. A picture of two beautiful, young girls appeared on the video screen. She turned away from looking at the video screen and faced the class once again.

"One of the biggest misconceptions is that honor killings only happen in the Middle East. This is not true. The brutal act of honor killings have come here to America."

Sakina paused and stared at the picture of the two young girls on the video screen. There was an eerie silence in the classroom. Sakina turned back again to face the class. Her eyes were filled with sadness.

" This is one of the last pictures taken of Amina and Sarah Said. A few days after this picture was taken, their father, Yaser, shot both of them to death in the back seat of his taxi cab."

There were audible gasps of horror. Some women turned their faces away and bowed their heads in despair.

"A 911 operator heard the chilling last desperate words of Sarah, bleeding to death from being shot, crying out on her cell phone, "Oh my God, I'm dying!"

A look of rage and anger came over Sakina's face.

"Why would a father do such a horrible thing to his own children?"

Sakina slammed her hand down on the lecture podium in disgust.

"Honor! He disapproved of their lifestyle. He had arranged for them to return to Egypt for a forced marriage and they both refused! They wanted to have American boyfriends instead and their choice cost them their lives!"

Another picture dissolved onto the video screen. It was the photo of a young 16 year-old girl named Tina.

" This is Tina, a 16 year-old Palestinian girl living in St. Louis, Missouri in 1989. Tina loved rap, R&B and rock music. She just wanted to enjoy life and have her own friends. She had taken a part-time job at McDonalds without her father's permission and was dating a non-Muslim, African-American man.

Unfortunately, her father disapproved of her choices and complained she had become "too westernized." Together, with her mother holding her down, her father Zein stabbed her to death."

Sakina shook her head in disgust and gazed back at the screen once again.

"My last example is the case of Noor Almakeli. Her father Faleh, struck and killed his daughter in a parking lot in Phoenix. He was angry that she had become too westernized by shunning an arranged marriage."

The lights came back on in the classroom. Sakina put her remote back down on the table.

" These are just a few stories. There are thousands more and in some cases, honor killings occur and are not reported."

Sakina took a sip of water and looked intently at the students in her class.

" Back in Pakistan, I remember a gruesome story of parents who killed their daughter with acid for just looking at another boy and they feared dishonor."

Gasps of disgust and horror could be heard throughout the classroom.

"If a woman is raped, she is treated like a criminal with no justice. The community fears that she had done something to provoke the attack and therefore she is stoned because her rape has brought dishonor."

Sakina bowed her head for a moment in order to collect her thoughts. Students noticed the pain and despair in her eyes.

"Before I show you the film, "Prisoner of her culture," which features interviews of women who managed to survive attempted honor killings, I first want to share with you a little bit more about myself.

When I was 16, I became a bride in a forced marriage. My husband Kamal was 19, three years older than I was. He is still my husband today. For the last nine years, I have lived under his strict control and domination. I must submit and obey every one of his demands. I do this out of fear for my life. Even though I live here in freedom, I cannot just walk away. If I did, my parents, my brothers, my family would hunt me down and then you'd be seeing my story in one of these films!"

Sakina paused and took a nervous deep breath.

" I live a dual life. My husband and family don't know anything about my human rights activities. I hide it from them. When I go home, I have to dress like I was back in Pakistan. My husband demands this! He hates the way women live here and how they dress. Yet he chose to live here because of the economic benefits, but he hates the culture.

The Muslim community here in Key West have shunned me. They believe that my lectures and the film that I show gives Islam a bad name and misrepresents their way of life. I have received numerous death threats for showing this film.

I share this way because I know what I'm talking about. I cannot keep silent. I believe my religion is a peaceful religion but there needs to be serious reform and change. I cannot keep silent and allow more innocent women to die. My dream is to have a 24 hour women's shelter and counseling center built all over the cities of America, where women can go to find help and safety.

As you watch this film, I ask that you would say a silent prayer for these innocent women and please consider getting involved yourself to put an end to these horrible honor killings. Thank you. Allah bless you.

****

After the film, Sakina took the time to answer questions and meet with the students who had attended the lecture. Shawn patiently waited at the side of the classroom until the crowds began to thin out. Sakina thanked each one of the students for coming and stood by herself next to the lap top waiting for Shawn to approach her.

Shawn slowly walked forward toward Sakina and nervously cleared his throat, a little shy and unsure of what to say.

"You are a very courageous lady," Shawn confidently said, admiring Sakina's beauty as she stood a foot away from her.

" Thank you kind sir. I appreciate you coming," Sakina replied enthusiastically.

There was a brief moment of silence as Shawn hesitated, shy and unsure of what to say next. Then he chuckled, stumbling over his words.

"I'm sorry. My name is Shawn. Shawn Ackerman."

Sakina gave Shawn a puzzled look trying to remember him and then suddenly her eyes lit up with excitement.

"Oh, Oh yes. You have the radio program and you took my call!"

"Yes," Shawn said smiling, feeling a little more relaxed. *"The radio is just a hobby for right now."*

"Shawn, is it okay to call you by your first name?" Sakina reluctantly asked.

"Yes, yes, of course!"

"Shawn. What exactly do you do? What is your job?"

Shawn was caught off guard by Sakina's question. He mumbled something out loud and chuckled, feeling a little uneasy.

"*Well,*" Shawn began, giving Sakina guilty smile, "*I used to design computer programs, but one day, not too long ago, I was fired.*"

"Oh no, I'm so sorry," Sakina blurted out, interrupting.

Shawn blushed, stumbling over his words, and then began to explain again.

"*I was fired, so I've become kind of a beach bum now and then a part-time radio host, and...*"

Shawn paused and reached into his coat pocket, pulling out a tiny glass bottle of Jack Daniel's whiskey.

"And I've become a very good friend to Mr. Jack Daniels!"

Shawn burst into laughter, proudly displaying the tiny bottle in front of Sakina. Sakina gave Shawn a puzzled and startled look. Shawn feeling embarrassed, quickly stuffed the bottle back into his shirt pocket.

"*Look Sakina, mam, I don't want to take up anymore of your time...*"

"*No. No,*" Sakina reassured Shawn, touching his shoulder with her hand, "*I appreciate what you did, having me on your radio program sir, and also by attending my lecture. You're not taking up my time. I have enjoyed our talk and we have something very important together in common.*"

Shawn gave Sakina a curious stare, unsure of what she meant.

"*You see, unfortunately, even living in freedom here in America, I still am not free. I'm still a prisoner of my culture. And you also are a prisoner, if I might say.*"

"What do you mean?" Shawn asked with a puzzled look on his face.

Sakina took a deep breath.

"You are a prisoner of your addiction." Sakina pointed toward his shirt pocket.

Shawn nervously looked down at his shirt pocket with a guilty expression on his face. He was at a loss for words. Then he quickly composed himself.

"I see what you mean. Well, maybe we can help each other. What do you think?"

Shawn was amazed at what he had just said, at the words that had just come out of his mouth. Sakina slowly nodded her head in agreement. Shawn was mesmerized by Sakina's beautiful blue eyes. He was impressed by the way that she carried herself, confident, polite, and respectful. Sakina held out her hand. Shawn hesitated, not sure if he should shake it.

"Relax Shawn," Sakina assured him, "As you can see," she said pointing toward her hair, *" I'm a very liberal Muslim woman. I don't wear the hijab. I believe women should have a choice, and it's okay to shake a Muslim woman's hand. I don't follow all of the "male-imposed" rules like I did when I was in Pakistan."*

Shawn relaxed and took a hold of Sakina's outstretched hand. A huge smile beamed out from his eyes.

"I'm very glad to hear that Sakina. You are indeed an amazing woman!"

"The Muslim community doesn't think so. They feel I'm being too critical of Islam and spreading lies that aren't true, but I tell them that true Islam doesn't kill or control women. I ask them why they are afraid to speak out. Why don't they care enough about women to change the laws and save their lives, but they won't join me. They're too afraid of an Imam issuing a fatwa against them, calling for their death."

"You mentioned your husband doesn't know what you do. How do you hide your secret life from him?"

Sakina took a deep breath and looked down in frustration.

" It's not easy, Shawn. I have to be careful."

"But why, why can't you just walk away, Sakina? This is America. You have a choice!"

Sakina picked up her lap top and purse. Shawn's questions were causing her to feel trapped. She was afraid of confronting her dual life.

"As I mentioned in my lecture, my family would hunt me down. They would find me and kill me. It's their duty. They have to be true to their honor code."

Sakina pulled her purse up over her shoulder. She was anxious to leave.

" Wait. Wait!" Shawn stopped her by putting his hand on her shoulder. Sakina froze, giving him a startled look. *"Please Sakina. Let me help you. I can support you. I would like to have you as a guest again on my radio program. We can talk about your lecture today."*

Sakina's face beamed with gratitude. Shawn reached down in his jacket pocket with excitement.

" Oh. I almost forgot. I bought you a little present for your lecture."

Sakina's eyes grew wide with excitement. She took the gift bag from Shawn's hand and quickly parted open the tissue. Suddenly her face got an astonished look on it. She held in her hand a beautiful blue cup with a picture of a yellow dandelion on it. Her hand began to tremble and she quickly laid the cup down on the table.

"I'm sorry. I'm sorry. Did I buy you the wrong thing?" Shawn nervously asked.

"No! No!" Sakina stuttered nervously, trying to avoid Shawn's question.

Immediately her mind drifted back to when she was 16 years old and living in Pakistan. She remembered going into the bathroom late one night to commit suicide in order to escape her arranged marriage. She membered as she lifted up the knife to plunge it in her abdomen that she was stopped by an incredible vision of a person claiming to be Jesus. Jesus had stopped her from committing suicide and explained to her that one day she would meet a man who would give her, her favorite flower. Sakina remembered Jesus's exact words, *"And then you will know that I am who I claim to be, your Creator and your God!"*

Sakina was astonished. She couldn't believe what her eyes were gazing upon right now. Shawn must be the man that Jesus had spoken to her about. He had given her a coffee cup with a design of her favorite flower on it. Sakina's heart sank. What would she do now? Is Jesus really right? Is he really who he claimed to be? Sakina became terribly afraid. Her heart was filled with anxiety. Today she had been confronted to examine the truth claims of her own religion and it was frightening!

Chapter Ten

Another Murder in Key West

The Lazy Greco was a very popular *Key West Island tropical bar* with an ocean front location on the legendary Duvall Street. Locals swarmed to the bar enjoying frozen daiquiris, fresh pizza, and mouth-watering peeled shrimp, especially on the weekend when they remained open into the wee hours of the morning, not closing until 3 am. Locals were treated to the usual entertainment of 25 tv monitors and the best in every style of music provided by a DJ.

After a long day at work at the dentist office, Kamal Paracha strolled into the Lazy Greco Bar. He had just finished talking to Sakina and informed her that he had an emergency case that would take several hours and would be home late, not to wait up for him.

The loud blaring sound of tvs greeted his ears as he walked up to the bar and sat down to relax. For a Thursday night, the crowd was pretty shallow. There were less than a hundred people, sitting in booths, drinking, smoking, and playing cards. The DJ was on a break, so the noise volume was now a little more tolerable.

Kamal was 6 ft. tall, thin, with a neatly trimmed black beard covering his face. He had just changed out of his dental uniform and was wearing a short sleeve tan shirt and gray-colored cacki pants. He felt much more comfortable and relaxed.

"Can I help you, sir?" the bartender asked, wiping the sweat from off of his brow.

"*Thanks. I'll wait,*" Kamal promptly replied.

He gazed around the bar. There was a couple and their friends, drinking and playing darts, having a good time. In the corner was another couple, holding hands with each other from across the table in a cozy booth, secluded in a dark corner away from the noise. A waitress arrived at their table, delivering a tasty seafood and shrimp feast in front of them. Kamal took a relaxing deep breath and spun back around on the bar stool. A few moments later, he felt the presence of someone walking up behind him. A short, black haired woman, dressed in a blue tank top and white shorts and tennis shoes, sat down next to Kamal at the bar. She plopped down her purse and began combing back her long black hair into a ponytail to be more comfortable.

Kamal was drawn to her sensuality and beauty. She was wearing heavy eye shadow and red lip stick. In the center of her chest, in the cleavage revealing the outline of her breasts was the picture of a red rose tattoo. Kamal gazed lustfully at her tattoo and was unaware that she had noticed him.

"*You like roses?*" the young lady asked, interrupting his gaze.

Kamal looked up in embarrassment, pretending that he wasn't staring at her tattoo.

"*Oh..Haaa,*" Kamal chuckled, "*Yes, roses are beautiful!*"

The beautiful young woman put an unlit cigarette between her lips. Right on cue, Kamal reached into his shirt pocket and lit her cigarette with his lighter. She quickly inhaled and blew the smoke in his face, laughing out loud.

"*Thank you,*" she hesitated and studied his face very carefully. "*I haven't seen you here before.*"

"*My name is Kamal.*"

"Sheila," Sheila abruptly answered back. Sheila noticed the olive-colored complexion of his face. *"Where are you from, Kamal?"*

"I'm from Pakistan. I moved here about two years ago."

Sheila nodded her head and held her cigarette in her left hand, relaxing on her bar stool.

"Pakistan," Sheila said with a puzzled look on her face, *" Well, welcome to our tropical paradise, where men get drunk and laid and party until they drop."*

The bartender interrupted their conversation by standing in front of them.

"Sheila, What would like tonight, my treat, ok?"

Sheila gave Kamal a smile of approval and took another puff on her cigarette.

"My favorite, a frozen daiquiri."

"Make that two," Kamal said to the bartender.

Sheila intently looked over inch of Kamal, her eyes wandering down his face all the way down to his belt buckle. She smacked her lips together with a sigh of pleasure and leaned closer to Kamal. Kamal could smell the exotic perfume Sheila was wearing. He was instantly aroused by the aroma.

"So Kamal," Sheila asked with a sensual tone in her voice, *" What do you do here in Key West?"*

Kamal took a deep breath. He could feel his body becoming sensually aroused from Sheila's perfume and mannerisms.

"I am a dentist." I have a local practice."

The bartender arrived back at their location, sitting down two frozen daiquiris in front of them. Sheila carefully stirred her daiquiri and took a quick sip.

"Ummm, Wow," Sheila groaned, her face broke out in a smile. *"A dentist?"* she chuckled, *"So you work in people's mouths for a living?"*

Sheila put down her drink, opened her mouth wide and leaned closer to Kamal, pressing her body up against his. Then she slid her hand down his leg and pressed it up against his zipper, slowly massaging him.

Kamal closed his eyes and slowly massaged Sheila's leg and then pressed his hand up against her abdomen.

"Let's go for a walk on the beach in the moonlight, ok?"

****

The ominous glow of the full moon illuminated the dark night, reflecting like a thousand diamonds on the waves of the Atlantic Ocean. It was a perfect romantic night for taking a lazy walk on South Beach. Sheila had drank a few too many daiquiris and was feeling rather tipsy right now. Kamal and Sheila had left the bar together and stopped at her car, removing their socks and shoes, preparing for a long and lazy walk on the beach.

It was 10:30 pm. They would have the beach all to themselves for as long as they wanted. Kamal took a hold of Sheila's hand. He could sense a strong sexual bond forming between them. Sheila stumbled, laughed and giggled, pulling Kamal into the foam of the waves that gently kissed the shoreline. They began splashing water in each other's faces, laughing, enjoying each other and then stopping to kiss, standing knee high in the ocean letting the surf splash up against their thighs.

Kamal gently rolled his tongue in Sheila's mouth, kissing her deeply. Sheila giggled and moaned, holding tightly onto Kamal, pressing her body up against his. They began walking toward the Duvall Street boardwalk that stretched out 100 feet into the ocean. Sheila took a relaxing deep breath and gazed at the moon, mesmerized by its magical glow.

"Do I turn you on, Kamal? Do I arouse you?" Sheila whispered sensually into his ear, gently nibbling on it with her lips.

Kamal stopped and lowered his head over Sheila's chest, gently gliding his tongue across the rose tattoo in the center. Sheila moaned with satisfaction as Kamal continued pleasing her chest tattoo with his tongue.

"Absolutely, you turn me on!" Kamal whispered back.

Sheila giggled and leaned her head back as Kamal gently moved his tongue up and down across the rose tattoo in the center of her chest.

"God, I want you!" Sheila moaned and then promptly pulled Kamal by his hand, running toward the boardwalk. The soft foam of the ocean waves splashed over their ankles as Sheila pulled Kamal underneath the boardwalk away from the glow of the moon. It was dark underneath the boardwalk except for the reflection of the moon glow on the ocean waves.

Sheila pulled Kamal up the hill in between the concrete boardwalk pillars, to a safe and soft spot on the sand. They were both standing up underneath the boardwalk just beyond the splash of the waves against the circular pillars.

Taking a deep breath, Sheila lifted up her tank top and pulled it over her head, exposing her breasts. Kamal moved closer and pulled her tightly up against his body and began deep mouth kissing her. Sheila groaned, enjoying every second of their passion. She maneuvered her right hand down Kamal's leg and found his zipper. She anxiously unzipped him and began vigorously massaging him with unrestrained passion.

Their passions intensified. Sheila pulled her mouth away and began sucking Kamal on his neck.

"Let's go back to my place," Sheila proposed, groaning and gasping for breath in the heat of their passion. Kamal groaned with satisfaction and slowly began to move around to Sheila's back, kissing her up and down her neck. He had positioned himself behind Sheila.

"I love this!" Sheila exclaimed, leaning her head back as Kamal kissed her passionately up and down her neck from behind her.

Suddenly she felt Kamal tighten his left hand sharply against her breast. She couldn't move, his grip was so strong. Then she felt the sharp blade of a knife cut vigorously across her jugular vein. Sheila tried to scream but couldn't. She began to suffocate, gasping for air, trying desperately to scream, but all she could do was gurgle. The blade of the knife had cut a deep incision across her neck. Blood began gushing out. Her heart began racing out of control. Sheila felt faint and numb and began losing consciousness. She finally dropped down to her knees and collapsed onto her side.

Kamal reached into his pocket and pulled out a glass vial. He knelt down and splashed the acid onto Sheila's face. She shrieked and her body convulsed, reacting to the intense burning on the skin of her face. Then after a few seconds, her whole body went limp and she stopped breathing, lying on her back with her eyes wide open.

The haunting sound of the ocean waves gently crashing onto the shoreline muffled the last desperate gasps of Sheila. Kamal put the glass vial back in his pocket and spit on Sheila's face.

"You whore," he bitterly said and quickly walked out from underneath the boardwalk back into the moonlight.

Chapter Eleven

A surprise visit from Pakistan

For the second afternoon in a row, the classroom had been filled to capacity with curious students, anxious to watch the film, "*Prisoner of her culture*." Sakina was overwhelmed by the responses of the students and very grateful to Shawn for faithfully promoting her lectures on his radio program.

Sakina spent more than 45 minutes after the film answering tough questions about her faith as a Muslim, her personal experience of being in an arranged marriage, and how she hid her activism from her husband. Today she was emotionally drained but encouraged that college students were becoming educated and aware of the horrible nature of honor killings. It had been a long afternoon and the last group of students walked out the door heading for their next class.

As Sakina finished packing up her lap top, she felt the presence of someone lurking in the corner of the room. Looking up from her lap top, Sakina noticed a tall, thin, beautiful black haired young girl standing a few feet away.

"*I'm sorry, Please come closer. How can I help you?*"

As the young girl drew closer, Sakina marveled at her beauty. Her black hair was beautifully styled and highlighted with amber brown streaks. She was very thin, petite and dressed in stylish blue jeans and silk pink blouse.

"*Thank you for coming,*" Sakina paused, unsure of her name.

"Samira. My name is Samira," Samira smiled, holding out her hand. Sakina warmly shook her hand and gazed intently into Samira's deep brown eyes.

"You are so lovely, Samira," Sakina said in a gracious tone of voice.

Samira blushed, unsure of what to say.

"Thank you Sakina. So are you."

Sakina pointed to a desk and Samira put her purse across her shoulder and sat down across from her. Samira relaxed and folded her hands, staring into Sakina's eyes.

"I want to thank you for your courage, Sakina, for not being afraid to break the silence, inspite of the whole Muslim community protesting against you!"

Sakina's face glowed with gratitude. She cleared her throat and began to speak.

"I *knew someone had to speak up. I lived in a culture of death for more than 20 years. Women tortured, killed, treated like cattle and bought and sold like slaves. I knew I had to be their voice!"*

Samira shook her head in agreement.

"How do you handle the death threats?"

Sakina took a deep breath and rolled her eyes.

"I'm used to it, Samira. But someone has to do it! My religion desperately needs reform but everyone is so afraid to speak up."

Samira bowed her head with a look of despair. Then she lifted her head back up, staring deeply into Sakina's eyes.

"I too am a Muslim like you Sakina. When I heard about the film, at first I was afraid to attend but then I heard your

interview on the radio and decided that now was the time. So I have come to support you."

"God bless you, Samira."

Samira turned her head away in shame. Sakina noticed the guilty look in her eyes.

"What's wrong, Samira?"

Samira glanced back at Sakina, struggling to compose herself.

"I'm like you Sakina. I choose not to wear the hijab. I believe Muslim women should have a choice."

"Yes! Yes!" Sakina enthusiastically agreed. Samira struggled to finish her thought.

"Sakina. I have to tell you something."

Sakina noticed the look of apprehension deep in Samira's eyes.

"It's ok," Sakina reassured her, *"I'm your friend."*

Samira shifted nervously in her chair and then mustered up the courage to speak.

"I'm beginning to doubt my Faith, Sakina. I-I-I'm not sure anymore. I'm beginning to doubt that Islam is really a religion of peace."

Samira's confession stunned Sakina. She quickly pretended to not be shaken by her honesty.

"You see, Sakina, that film you showed is filled with too many horror stories. All that you hear about in the news from ISIS to Charlie Hebdo killings, is that "radical" Muslims were responsible, but..but," Samira stuttered nervously, *"I don't believe that anymore. I don't see a distinction. I believe Islam is Islam."*

Sakina was shaken by Samira's honesty. She sat quietly listening, desperately searching for an answer. Finally Sakina managed to think of a reply.

" Well. The Quran doesn't teach that, Samira. There are radicals who have deliberately hijacked our religion!"

Samira shook her head in protest. Tears filled her eyes.

" I understand Sakina. I believed that at one time too, but when I read the Quran, I now understand that Islam is really not peaceful, even according to its own holy book!"

Sakina had a startled look on her face. Samira wiped the tears off of her face.

" For example, The Quran commands the husband to beat his own wife. In Surah 4:34, The Quran declares that, "men are superior to women, and if a husband suspects his wife of infidelity, he must first, confront her and if that doesn't bring about a change, then he is instructed not to sleep with her, and if she still doesn't listen, the husband must beat her until she repents or has a change of heart.

Sakina, women are treated like second class citizens in Islam. They must obey their husbands without question."

As Samira made her case, Sakina meditated silently on the many times Kamal had abused her and physically beat her. She remained quiet. She could offer no reply to Samira.

"Also in the Hadith, which many Muslims accept as the sayings and teachings of the prophet Mohammed, Mohammed is quoted as declaring, "If any man changes his religion, kill him!" (Bukhari 89:271)

Sakina, this contradicts the early teachings of the Quran, which taught, "there is no compulsion in religion," (Surah 2:256). Yet here we have our prophet forbidding any Muslim from choosing to leave Islam, and if they do, a fatwa, a death warrant is placed over their head.

Sakina, where is the peace? Where is the tolerance? "Slay the infidels (kill them) wherever you find them," (Surah 2:191-193) Our Holy book teaches these things and when I understood it, I could no longer be a Muslim. Do you understand, Sakina?"

Sakina nervously swallowed. She could see the conviction and passion in Samira's eyes. She struggled for an answer.

"Samira, Isn't this just your interpretation of the Quran? Have you asked an Imam about these verses or did you just decide on your own?"

Samira rolled her eyes in frustration.

"Sakina. I admire and respect you. You are one of the most courageous Muslim women that I've ever met. I'm asking you as a friend. Please take one more step of courage, read the Quran just like I did and carefully read the verses and I believe you too will come to the same conclusion. Trust your instincts as woman, Sakina. Don't let another man tell you what to believe!"

Sakina realized that she could not change Samira's mind. She sat quietly absorbing everything that Samira had said. Exhausted and out of answers, Sakina wanted to flee. She made a quick excuse to leave.

"It's getting late I must go," Sakina explained.

Samira gave Sakina an understanding smile, offering to walk out the door with her. They both walked out together into the bright sunlight. As they descended down the steps of the front entrance, Sakina abruptly stopped. Two Muslim men in black beards and a young Muslim woman stood at the bottom of the steps, staring at them with angry faces.

"Samira. Don't let that evil woman corrupt your mind," the young angry Muslim woman warned her with a fierce and vengeful look in her eyes. *" What right have you to poison our religion by showing a film full of lies?"* The Muslim man asked with a bitter and antagonistic tone in his voice.

"Have you seen the film?" Sakina asked, challenging the Muslim man.

" No, I won't watch that filth!"

"It's blasphemous, what you are doing!" The Muslim woman interrupted.

Sakina was losing her patience. She sternly looked at the Muslim man and woman.

" When will you stop attacking me and instead join me in confronting the radicals who are giving a bad name to our religion with their honoring killings and forced marriages?

Our religion needs reform. Instead of attacking me, join with me and let's put a stop to the abuse and murder of our women!"

"I don't care about your film. What I care about is how you are indoctrinating and changing the minds of Muslim women. You have succeeded in changing Samira's mind and now like you, she refuses to wear her hijab!"

"I didn't change her mind!" Sakina snapped back, *"She has a choice. She chose not to wear the hijab and that is her choice. The Quran doesn't teach what you say. That's just your interpretation!"*

Samira remained quiet, standing close to Sakina. Sakina put her arm around Samira to protect her.

" Stop treating Muslim women like slaves. They are human beings not puppets, who must fall in line like mindless victims!"

The Muslim woman, her eyes filled with anger and resentment, stepped up closer to Sakina and pointed her finger in her face.

"You are putting yourself and Samira in grave danger. I am warning you!"

Sakina pulled Samira by the hand and quickly walked past the group of angry Muslims. She realized the danger of breaking the silence and the angry confrontation only served to strengthen her faith and passion for speaking the truth.

The day that Sakina dreaded had finally arrived. Friday morning Kamal had returned from the airport bringing Sakina's parents home from Pakistan to stay with them for the next month. Sakina hadn't seen Akbar and Ayesha for almost nine years and that was fine with her! She knew they only had come to see Kamal. Their world revolved around Kamal, specifically because he was a man and in their eyes, was a very successful son-in-law to have graduated from Dental School and started his own business. For Sakina, their visit for the next month was only more mouths to feed and longer hours in the kitchen. The next month would not only be exhausting for Sakina, but also more stressful. She had three more lectures scheduled and film showings at another nearby college that Shawn had arranged for her through his radio program. With her parents in town, she had to be extra careful and cleverer as to not give away her secret dual life as a human rights activist.

****

Akbar dabbed his lips with a napkin after finishing a plate of delicious breaded shrimp and crab cakes. Streaks of gray filled his black beard and a few wrinkles were beginning to form on the cheeks of his face. Ayesha smiled toward Sakina as she took a sip of tea. She relaxed back in her chair.

"*Very good, Sakina,*" Ayesha said, complimenting her daughter.

"*She is a good cook,*" Kamal agreed, as he wiped his mouth with his napkin and took a quick sip of tea.

Akbar relaxed comfortably back in his chair and stared at Kamal. His eyes beamed with joy as he gazed at his son-in-law. Then he quickly lifted his glass in the air to propose a toast.

"I propose a special toast to you Kamal, my wonderful son-in-law. You have made me very proud!"

Kamal blushed a little and nodded his head in gratitude and respect toward Akbar.

" Thank you sir."

"Thank you Kamal for paying for our plane tickets and allowing us to stay at your beautiful condo," Ayesha said respectfully.

" It is my pleasure. I'm sure Sakina is very happy to cook for you both and now you can see what a wonderful housewife she has become."

Sakina kept quiet and looked down at the table. Her soul was raging with bitterness. She hated the stigma of being classified as a "glorified" housewife, while Kamal received praise for his dental career. Sakina was tired of being a slave and a second-class citizen.

" So you like it here in America, Kamal?" Akbar asked.

Kamal took a deep breath. He had a perplexed look in his eyes.

" Well of course, the money is much better here. I love my practice, but," Kamal admitted, squirming in his chair, his face becoming red with anger. *" The problem I have living in America is that there is too much freedom."*

Both Akbar and Ayesha gave Kamal their full attention. Their eyes were riveted on every word he spoke. They treated him like a god.

" What is your complaint, son?" Akbar inquired.

Kamal cleared his throat. He briefly glanced over at Sakina and then stared back at Akbar and Ayesha.

"America needs Sharia law, father. The problems here would be quickly solved if the people understood that their actions brought severe consequences. The women here have too much freedom. They have no modesty in the way that they dress. They roam the streets half naked, with ugly tattoos all over their bodies and especially on the beach, they are barely dressed, inviting the lusts of men...It's disgusting!"

Akbar nodded his head in agreement.

"Women here have jobs and careers and are never home to take care of their husbands and children. They dress like whores and act like sluts...it's very disgusting!" Kamal bitterly complained, throwing his napkin down on the table.

Sakina couldn't resist any longer. She inhaled and took an angry deep breath.

"Excuse me, but I love the freedom here! Here women are treated equal to men. Here women have a real life and they are free to make choices and not be afraid like I was in Pakistan," Sakina protested with an angry tone in her voice.

Akbar's eyes widened in shock.

"Sakina. I am ashamed of you! How dare you speak up like that and disagree with your husband. I agree with everything that Kamal has just said!"

Sakina stood up and began gathering up the dishes. She slammed the dishes together in her hands, humiliated and angry at the way her father had spoken to her.

"I guess it's time for the maid to clean up," Sakina shouted sarcastically with her arms full of dishes. She promptly left the room and headed into the kitchen. She couldn't tolerate another minute of being treated like a slave. She realized it was going to be a very long and grueling month!

Chapter Twelve

"The Frantic Call at Midnight"

Shawn opened his eyes. He was lying on his back, half-dressed, his shoes and socks strewn on the floor. He sat up on the couch and rubbed his aching head. The last thing that he remembered was gulping down the rest of the bottle of Jack Daniels and then he passed out. He gazed around the room. The tv was still playing. *Fox and Friends* had just begun. It was 6 am.

Shawn gazed down at the floor. Pieces of cold pizza, paper plates, scotch toweling and paper from the printer was scattered all across the hardwood floor. His condo was a complete disaster. His lifestyle had become that of a drunken beach bum, part-time radio host and now a dedicated alcoholic!

Shawn fell back down on the couch and rubbed his unshaven face. His breath was appalling. He hadn't showered for now going on two days. He was disgusted with himself. He rubbed his eyes and took a deep breath. Just 1 month ago he was traveling across the country giving seminars on the latest cell phone for Global Vision. At that time he was one of the company's top computer software designers. But now he had gone from a successful professional at the height of his career to a disgusting alcoholic! Shawn had descended into the dark and unforgiving world of addiction.

Sitting up once again, Shawn bowed his head over his legs. He began to weep. Bitter tears filled his eyes as he remembered how life had been a sweet fulfilling adventure. He sat up on the edge of the couch, broken, desperate, and searching for a way out. Lifting his head up for a moment, his eyes fell upon the bookcase in the corner of the living room. Shawn had always loved to read, Sci-Fi, murder mysteries and stories from the Bible. He still loved the feel and smell of real books that he could hold in his hands and turn the pages.

Getting up from the couch, Shawn stumbled across the floor, his feet slipping on the pizza slices and paper plates. He struggled to keep his balance, still hungover from the lonely party the night before. Reaching into the bookcase, he pulled out his leather Bible and dusted off the cover. He didn't know exactly why, but he felt the urge to read his Bible that he hadn't touched in over two years since he began his new career. This morning he needed answers! His heart was crying out for help. He remembered Sakina's words, *"You are a prisoner like me, except you are a prisoner to your own addiction!"*

Shawn returned to the couch and sat down. Opening up the Bible, he flipped through the pages, unsure of what to read, but knowing he needed to hear the voice of God right now. His finger landed on Jeremiah Chapter 31. He gazed down at verse 3.

"I have loved you my people, with an everlasting love. With unfailing love, I have drawn you to myself."

That one sentence, that one statement and declaration seemed to awaken Shawn and breathe life back into him once again. It was as if God himself had just pulled him up out of the dark pit and washed him clean of all of the dirt and mess. It was as if Jesus had touched his eyes to see for the first time, awakening him from a lifelong blindness. *"I have loved you with an everlasting love!"*

Shawn bowed his head and burst into tears. Was it really possible that God still loved him? Did he still love him after all of the day and nights he had sold his soul to alcohol? Falling to his knees, Shawn wept, moaning like a frightened child, desperately afraid because he had become separated from his dad.

"Oh God," Shawn lamented, *"Oh God, please help me! Please save me! Please forgive me!"*

Almost immediately, Shawn felt a river of liquid love pour all over his body, cleansing him, purging him of every sin and every wrong doing. His whole body was absorbed in radiant heat, a burning sensation of unconditional love cleansing his entire being. When he opened his eyes again, he felt completely whole and delivered. His kissed his Bible in tears and stood up, only this time, he didn't stumble or stagger. He felt totally rejuvenated and completely set free. Seeing the bottles of Jack Daniels laying on the floor, Shawn grabbed them up in his hands and threw them into the garbage can. Then he raised his arms up into the air, rejoicing loudly, "*I am free! I am free!*" Shawn pulled out his cell phone and speed dialed Nabeel's number. He couldn't wait to share the good news with him!

****

"*Brother, I'm so excited that you have come back to us!*" Nabeel exclaimed, tightly hugging Shawn.

Tears of joy filled Shawn's eyes. After a few moments of rejoicing they both sat down together on the couch.

"*Please forgive me for this messy house,*" Shawn said in embarrassment.

"*No. Don't worry,*" Nabeel reassured him. "*The most important this is that you are back! You've come home again just like the prodigal son did.*"

Shawn wiped the tears from off of his face.

"*I'm free, Nabeel! I'm no longer a prisoner!*"

"*Amen! Amen!*" Nabeel agreed.

Shawn turned and faced Nabeel. His face beamed with joy.

"Nabeel. When I met Sakina, I knew almost right away, I had found my purpose in life. It all fit together. The night I went to church with David and heard you speak, something inside of me snapped. Even though I was anxious to leave, something inside of me connected to those suffering Christians in Pakistan."

Shawn paused. His face radiated with joy.

"And then I met Sakina! Sakina's story of abuse and suffering brought me right back to the suffering Christians in Pakistan and your incredible testimony. Nabeel, I knew I had found my purpose. Before, I was selfish, absorbed into the world of technology, committed to wealth and security. Then God pulled the rug out underneath my world and when I met Sakina, I knew I had to help her. I knew I had to be her voice and voice of suffering Muslim women in Pakistan!"

Nabeels' eyes grew wide with joy and excitement.

"Shawn. The Lord has put this woman in your life. I believe he did shake your world. He took away your job, your security, your wealth, and replaced it with a greater calling. He has made you a compassionate voice, a voice of hope for abused women like Sakina."

"Nabeel. I didn't realize that I was fighting against God. I decided to go to church that night and the very thing that I was fighting against has turned out to be the greatest blessing in my life!"

Nabeel tightly hugged Shawn again.

"My dear brother. God is about to take you on the greatest adventure of your life!"

****

A loud ringtone awakened Shawn out of a deep sleep. He reached over to grab his cellphone.

"*Hello,*" he answered, half-asleep, in a groggy voice.

"*Shawn! Please come quick!*" The frantic voice urged him.

"*Sakina!*"Shawn quickly sat up in bed, recognizing her voice.

"*He's beat me!*"Sakina said in a moaning voice.

" *Where are you?*" Shawn asked in a panicked voice, sitting up on the edge of the bed.

" *The Lazy Greco Bar. Please come quickly. I'm scared!*"

"*I'll be there in five minutes,*" Shawn promised, as he threw on his pants. He quickly disconnected the call.

****

Shawn flung open the front door to the Lazy Greco Bar on Duvall Street. There were a few guests sitting at the bar. The tv was playing at a low volume and the main lobby was empty like a ghost town. Shawn frantically ran past the bar, looking in the booths until he finally saw Sakina, standing up out of the shadows against the wall in the corner, secluded from all of the noise. Shawn raced toward Sakina and threw his arms around her. Sakina burst into tears and pressed her head tight against his shoulder.

"*It was awful! He almost killed me!*" Sakina cried out in a trembling voice.

Shawn quickly pulled away and examined Sakina's face. She had cuts and bruises on her cheek bone and a black eye. Her hair was a matted mess and her eyes were swollen and tear-soaked.

Shawn's face grew red with rage.

"That bastard! Why did he do this?"

Shawn gently helped Sakina to sit down in a booth. Sakina wiped her face off and struggled to compose herself. She couldn't stop shaking from fear.

"My parents had just left the condo to go to bed," Sakina explained. Shawn put his arm around Sakina and dabbed the wounds on her face with his handkerchief. Sakina flinched in pain.

"You see, Kamal insisted that they have their own beach house to stay at and relax and sleep peacefully at night."

Sakina banged her fist down on the table. She stared at Shawn with a raged look in her eyes.

"Now I know why he insisted on them having a private beach house at night. So he could secretly abuse me!"

A waitress came to the table interrupting their conversation. Shawn ordered two cups of coffee. Then he continued to dab Sakina's wounds with a handkerchief. Sakina took a nervous deep breath and brushed her hair, dropping her head in despair.

"This afternoon, I spoke my mind to him in front of my parents. I told him women here have freedom, they have choices. Kamal resented that I dare disagree with him in front of his in laws. So tonight he approached me as I was getting ready for bed and began yelling at me. When I tried to walk away, he-."

Sakina's voice cracked with emotion. Tears filled her swollen eyes. Shawn pulled her head against his shoulder.

"First he slapped me, and then punched me. I screamed. Then he grabbed me and tried to strangle me. When I finally broke away, he punched me again and again, until I fell on the

floor. I found his shoe on the floor and hurled it at him. That gave me time to get up and run out of the door."

Sakina broke down in tears again. The trauma had overwhelmed her. The waitress arrived with the two coffees. Shawn smiled graciously at the waitress and gave her a twenty dollar tip.

"Here. Please take a sip."

Shawn gently guided the cup of coffee toward her lips and Sakina slowly sipped it. After a few moments, she became calmer.

"Sakina," Shawn said.

Sakina looked up and saw a defiant look in Shawn's eyes.

"You are not going to become another honor killing statistic. I refuse to let you become another statistic!"

Sakina took a frustrating deep breath. She had a confused and perplexed look on her face.

"I'm trapped! What can I do? If I call the police, he will kill me!"

Sakina turned her head away in desperation. Shawn gently pulled her closer to him.

"Sakina. Tonight I prayed to Jesus and he delivered me from alcohol. I am no longer a prisoner!"

Sakina's face changed from despair to joy.

"Oh Shawn, I'm so happy for you!"

"Sakina," Shawn interrupted. His eyes were riveted on Sakina with a look of compassion.

"You too are going to be set free!"

"What do you mean?" Sakina asked.

Shawn edged closer to Sakina.

"You are going to take Kung Fu classes."

Sakina gazed at Shawn with an astonished look in her eyes.

"What?" she abruptly asked.

"Kung Fu classes. I know an excellent instructor. He has a studio just a few blocks away from here and he is one of the best."

"Are you serious?" Sakina blurted out with a perplexed look on her face. *"Shawn, I can't do that!"*

"Yes you can and you will!" Shawn snapped back. *"Jesus delivered me from my prison and he will do the same for you!"*

Sakina could see the determination and love in Shawn's eyes. For the first time in her life, she felt loved and protected. The thought of defending herself was frightening. Sakina had lived in a prison of fear all of her life, but tonight Shawn had said something powerful to her, which struck a chord deep down in her heart, *"You're not going to be another statistic!"*

Those words from Shawn were life changing. Inspite of being afraid, Sakina began to believe what Shawn had just told her.

Chapter Thirteen

Another Acid Attack

Sakina held tightly onto Samira's hand. Samira's face was completely bandaged except for a small section above her nose for her eyes to look out of. An *IV* line for antibiotics was inserted into her right arm and connected to a pump next to her bed. Samira laid completely still, her eyes gazing out from behind the bandages, staring aimlessly ahead without feeling or emotions. She was physically alive but spiritually dead, numb and completely detached from the world around her.

The last thing she remembered was a man emerging from the dark shadows of an alley way and throwing acid onto her face. The pain and trauma had been so severe that Samira collapsed her face on fire and her body trembling and shaking from the gruesome attack. Sakina fought back the tears. She wanted to be strong for her friend. She had just finished her lecture when a friend of Samira's had broken the news to her about the terrible attack. Sakina politely dismissed herself from the students who had stayed to ask questions and immediately rushed to the hospital.

Sakina gripped Samira's hand tightly and leaned closer to her bandaged face. Samira remained completely still, not uttering a sound, but staring straight ahead, immune to her presence in the room.

"Samira," Sakina tenderly whispered*, "I am here with you dear friend."*

Sakina could feel a slight twinge from Samira's hand as if she was awakening. A tiny tear dribbled onto the bandages below her eyes. Sakina leaned closer until she was almost directly over her face.

"I want to die!" Sakina finally blurted out with a bitter tone in her voice.

Sakina gripped Samira's hand as tight as she could. Tears filled her eyes. She reached across with her right arm, hugging Samira tightly.

"I want to die!" Samira screamed once again. Sakina held on tightly to her best friend.

"I love you! I love you!" Sakina proclaimed, her voice cracking with emotion.

After composing herself, Sakina looked intently at Samira.

" Who did this to you?"

Samira began shaking with fear.

" I don't know...I don't know," Samira bitterly wept. *"All I remember is leaving the café and walking through the alley way to the parking lot when a man rushed out of the darkness. I couldn't see his face. He demanded, "Where is your hijab?"*

I stopped, afraid and astonished. Before I could utter a reply, I suddenly felt...."

Sakina paused, overwhelmed with fear and anxiety.

" This incredible burning sensation all over my face. The pain was so unbelievable. I just collapsed and..."

Samira turned over on her left side, pulling away from Sakina's hug and broke down in tears again. Sakina felt helpless, unable to comfort her friend. She was shocked that a vicious acid attack, like the ones she remembered while living in Pakistan, were happening here in Florida. *What kind of demented maniac would target Muslim women here*? Sakina pondered quietly to herself.

For the first time since she left Pakistan, Sakina was terribly afraid for her life once again.

****

Detective Williams sat with his partner Bill Ronson at the Lazy Greco Bar on Duvall Street. The receipt found in the pocket of Sheila Watson had led them to the last place where she was seen alive. The receipt was for $12.50 and was time stamped at 9:45 pm. The time was very important. It helped to establish the approximate time of her death. Sheila's gruesome body had been discovered underneath the boardwalk at 4 am by some young teenagers out past their curfew. Her throat had been slit and her face disfigured by an apparent acid attack.

Joe the bartender emerged from out of the kitchen and stood in the cubicle behind the counter.

"May I help you gentlemen?"

"I'm Detective Williams and this is my partner, Detective Ronson. We're investigating the death of Sheila Watson."

Detective Williams showed the receipt to the bartender. As he was reading the time stamp, Detective Ronson displayed a photograph of Sheila. Joe took photograph from Detective Ronson's hand and examined it carefully.

"Yeah, yeah! I remember her. She was kind of a regular here."

Joe thought carefully for a moment.

"Yeah, it was Thursday around 9 pm."

He handed the photograph back to Detective Ronson.

" Was she alone?"

Joe took a deep breath and thought for a moment.

" Yeah. She came in alone and sat down here and struck up a conversation with a guy."

"Do you remember what he looked like?"

"Ah," Joe stuttered, trying to recall. *"He was new to this place. I've never seen him before. I remember he had olive-colored skin, like he was "middle-eastern."*

Detective Williams turned and gave his partner a perplexed look.

" Middle-eastern?"

" Yeah. He had a neatly trimmed black beard, as best as I can remember."

"Did Sheila meet him for the first time or did she know him?"

Joe thought carefully.

"It seems like they had first met, the way they talked to one another."

"You say, you never saw him before?" Detective Ronson inquired.

Joe shook his head.

" Never saw him before Thursday night."

A series of ringtones interrupted their conversation. It was Detective William's cellphone ringing.

" Detective Williams," Ron answered.

He listened carefully for a few minutes.

"Thank you very much, Mr. Aguilar."

Detective Williams returned his cell phone to his belt clip.

"That was a Mr. Agular. He called the tip line to say he recognized the dead girl's picture as the person he recognized sitting at the bar Thursday night and he added, the person she was talking to was his dentist! Apparently they recognized the man at the bar because his wife is a patient of his."

Detective Williams turned his attention back to Joe the bartender.

"Thank you Joe. You've been very helpful. Here's my card if you remember anything else."

Detective Williams and Bill Ronson both left the Lazy Greco and headed back toward their vehicle.

"The name of the dentist is Dr. Kamal Paracha and he is definitely a middle-eastern man!"

"Wow!" Detective Ronson exclaimed, *"So what do you think?"*

Detective Williams opened the car door.

"Well at this point. I think we need to pay Dr. Paracha an important visit and it's not for a checkup."

Detective Ronson chuckled and sat down in the passenger side of their police car. Detective Williams adjusted his rear view mirror.

"Both of these homicides have a distinct pattern of the use of acid to disfigure the victim's faces. You hear about that sort of thing happening in the Middle East."

"And Dr. Paracha is Middle-Eastern," Detective Ronson pointed out.

"*Exactly!*" Detective Williams agreed. "*Let's pay the good doctor a quick visit, shall we?*"

Chapter Fourteen

A Sunset to Remember

Mallory Square Plaza, at the waterfront, where one could gaze out into the beautiful and majestic ocean waters of the Gulf of Mexico, was the location of the famous "sunset celebration." Each night, both locals and tourists, came together for a festival celebration, two hours before sunset. The Waterfront plaza was filled with food carts, booths, fire jugglers, musicians and people walking their dogs. The evening culminated with a breathtaking experience of watching the pink and red colors of a gorgeous sunset, graciously melting below the horizon in the Gulf of Mexico.

Kamal had just left for Denver, Colorado to attend a three-day dentist convention leaving Sakina alone for the first time. It was the perfect occasion for Shawn and her to spend some time together and get to know each other better. Shawn suggested that they spend the evening at Mallory Square and celebrate the gorgeous sunset. It would be Sakina's first experience at the Sunset Celebration.

****

It was 6 pm when Shawn and Sakina arrived at the crowded waterfront in Mallory Square. Already a sizeable crowd had gathered anticipating a wonderful, fun filled and romantic evening, connecting with food and nature's display of splendor.

As they strolled onto the boardwalk together, the quiet and relaxing sound of a guitarist gently strumming some beautiful chords, greeted their ears. Sakina was wearing a pink tank top and cutoff jeans and sandals, perfect clothing for the celebration. She pushed her black sunglasses down over her eyes and breathed in the moist tropical air coming from the Gulf of Mexico.

Shawn reached down to give a biscuit treat to a beautiful tan and white, border collie dog. Sakina knelt down and talked to a 2 year-old boy with his father, walking their dog.

"You are so cute!" Sakina said with joy in her eyes, wishing she too could one day get pregnant and have her own child.

A large crowd had gathered near the end of the boardwalk facing the Gulf of Mexico. A fire juggler, sitting on a tall steel bicycle seat, was dazzling his audience by keeping his balance while tossing fiery batons into the air and catching them with pin point accuracy without being burned.

Sakina and Shawn applauded loudly, fascinated by the juggler's amazing skill. The tempting smell of Gyros cooking in the distance drew Shawn and Sakina to a nearby food cart. Delicious ground lamb, garlic, onions and tzatziki sauce on a pita bread, was an awesome Greek sandwich that was simply tantalizing to the taste buds!

They found a quiet resting place on a bench overlooking the railing with a magnificent view of the Gulf of Mexico. It was a seaside place away from the noise of the crowd, where the lapping sound of the ocean beating against the dock, could be heard with the occasional "crowing" sound of the seagulls soaring overhead.

Sakina and Shawn both sat down wooden bench and leaned back soaking in the beautiful sun and connecting with the hypnotic sound of the ocean waves kissing the waterfront. Shawn took a big bite of his gyro and moaned with satisfaction.

"Oh Shawn, this is like paradise," Sakina happily said, taking a deep breath and closing her eyes connecting with the sounds of the ocean. *" What a good idea you had!"*

Shawn smiled towards Sakina and took a gulp of lemonade. Then he gently pushed the lemonade cup up against Sakina's lips, while she took a refreshing drink.

" Thank you," Sakina said with a relaxed smile on her face.

Up and down the boardwalk were several lamp posts that would shine brilliantly once the sunset had finally arrived. Sakina finished her gyro and then bent down to remove her sandals. Then she leaned back, relaxing on the bench, stretching her legs across Shawn's lap.

"Do you mind, Shawn?" Sakina quietly asked, laying her head back on the bench and completely relaxing.

"Not. Not at All!" Shawn replied, smiling as he gently massaged Sakina's feet. *"I want you to relax and forget about everything. This is our special evening together."*

Sakina gave Shawn a look of gratitude and turned to gaze out at the ocean.

"I could lie here all day and just absorb the beauty and majesty of the ocean," Sakina said in a relaxing reflection. Then she looked back at Shawn.

"I'm so proud of you, Shawn for being alcohol free! You're no longer a prisoner to your addiction!"

Shawn smiled and pushed his sunglasses over his eyes and stared out toward the ocean.

"Sakina. I owe it all to you!"

"Me?" Sakina said with a puzzled look on her face.

"Yes. When I first met you and heard your story, I knew right away that I had found my purpose in life."

Shawn looked down at Sakina, massaging her bare leg.

"Your purpose?" Sakina answered with a perplexed look on her face.

" Yes. I knew I had to be your voice, to be a voice for the other voiceless women who were suffering in Pakistan. You story and the stories of the women you shared, struck a chord in my soul. Most of my life, I have been so self-centered, focused on my career, my money, my reputation..."

Shawn paused and bowed his head in shame.

" When I saw the faces of the women whose lives had been shattered, I broke inside."

Sakina was overwhelmed with gratitude. Her eyes began to fill with tears. She sat up and moved closer toward Shawn.

" Shawn, you are an angel of God, that He sent to me."

Shawn raised his head back up and gazed intently into Sakina's blue eyes.

" Losing my career was truly God's blessing, Sakina, because it brought you to me."

Sakina chuckled, wiping the tears from her eyes. *"Yes. I'm so grateful, Shawn."*

"I knew I had to use all of my energy and skills to help you, to promote your lectures on my radio program and that required a sober mind. So one morning, I finally saw clearly the dark hole alcohol had trapped me in and I asked Jesus to deliver me and he did!" Shawn exclaimed.

Sakina gazed back toward the ocean, silently reflecting on what Shawn had shared with her.

" Shawn. I want to share something really incredible with you. I vividly remembered while I was living in Pakistan, more than 9 years ago, I had received the devastating news that my sister Mahtab had committed suicide."

"Oh no, I'm so sorry," Shawn blurted out, interrupting.

"Thank you," Sakina gratefully replied.

"That night, I didn't care anymore. I didn't want to become like my sister. I was tired of being controlled and abused, so while Kamal was sleeping, I crept into the bathroom, taking a knife, and was going to commit suicide, when..."

Sakina's face glowed with joy and excitement. *"I had a vision of a man in blazing white. He claimed to be Jesus.*

"Wow!" Shawn exclaimed.

"He stopped me just as I was about to plunge the knife in my abdomen and proclaimed, "Don't Sakina. I am your God and savior and I am your friend. I was stunned Shawn, because Muslims believe Jesus is only a prophet and in this vision, Jesus revealed himself as God! Then he told me, one day you will meet a man who will give you your favorite flower and then you will know that I am who I claimed to be!"

"The cup!" Shawn shouted in astonishment.

"Yes! Remember you gave me a cup at my lecture? It was a gift and on the side of the cup was a design of a yellow carnation, my favorite wildflower!"

Shawn's eyes grew wide in astonishment. He gazed intently as Sakina.

"That is incredible! Jesus gave you a sign, a prophecy and it came true!"

Sakina's face was flushed white in shock.

Shawn looked deeply into her blue eyes. *"Do you now believe?"*

Sakina nervously bit her lip in apprehension. Her faith had been challenged. She didn't know how to respond.

"As I sit here telling you this Shawn, I cannot deny the incredible peace that I feel. I don't know what to say!"

"Sakina," Shawn excitedly said, *"Jesus completely transformed my life. He took away the "demons" of alcohol that held me captive."*

Sakina nodded her head in agreement.

"Jesus loves you, Sakina. He has a perfect plan and purpose for your life. Now I know exactly why we met. Jesus will protect you Sakina. I promise to take you to the martial arts classes and you will be trained. You will never become another honor killing statistic. I promise you!"

"You truly are my angel, Shawn!" Sakina said, her face glowing with gratitude. Then, in an instant, she looked away and turned to face the ocean.

" What's wrong?" Shawn inquired.

" The acid murders," Sakina answered with a troubled look on her face. *" This demon, this deranged person. It reminds me of when I lived in Pakistan, but here, I don't understand."*

"What do you mean?" Shawn asked.

Sakina gazed back at Shawn with a frightened look on her face.

"I can't help but to speculate that this person is a middle-eastern man."

Shawn nodded his head in agreement. Sakina had a grim look on her face.

"Shawn. I'm afraid."

Shawn put his arm around Sakina. She laid her head on his shoulder.

"Kamal says terrible things about the women here. He hates the way they dress. He calls them sluts!"

Shawn held Sakina tighter.

"He's late coming home sometimes. He calls me saying that he has an emergency case. I'm in bed by the time he gets home."

"What are you trying to say, Sakina?"

Sakina lifted her head off of Shawn's shoulder. Her eyes were filled with fear.

"I-I," Sakina nervously stuttered, *"I'm afraid."*

****

The glowing lights coming from the lampposts along the waterfront, signaled the approaching sunset. Sakina and Shawn walked to the end of the pier and sat down with the crowd of people gathered to watch an incredible sunset. The fire jugglers had finished their performance and the carnival had packed up their toys until another night. The food and craft vendors were now closed for the evening and had joined the large crowd gathered at the end of the pier.

Shawn and Sakina sat down at the edge of the pier platform and let their bare feet dangle just above the ocean tide. A tiny sailboat glided across the sparkling waves toward the horizon. Brilliant pink and orange cloud formations arced across the sky as the sun, in a majestic glowing orange ball, slowly dipped below the horizon. Everyone's eyes were riveted upon the incredible display of colors bursting over the horizon. Nature was putting on a breath taking display of romantic beauty.

Shawn gently wrapped his left arm around Sakina. Sakina moved closer, resting her head on his shoulder. An incredible peace came over Shawn. He knew when he first gazed into Sakina's beautiful blue eyes that she was the one meant for him.

He desperately wanted to rescue her from a life of hell and treat her the way a real man should.

As the dazzling pink and orange colors began to fade below the horizon, Sakina lifted up her head and gazed deeply into Shawn's eyes. Shawn gently touched her lips with his. Then embracing her tighter, he began passionately kissing Sakina, unrestrained and unconcerned by who was watching. Sakina didn't resist but responded by wrapping her arms around Shawn's neck. Their souls seem to meet in the passion of the moment. For the first time in her life, Sakina felt loved and protected. Her anxiety and pain melted away as the sun sank below the horizon. The feeling of true love washed over her soul. Tonight, the blazing fire of true love had been born in her heart and Sakina had hope of finally breaking free from her prison of fear.

Chapter Fifteen

A Trip to the Dentist

It had been an extremely busy day for Kamal at the dentist office. Ten patients, six cleanings, three fillings and one extraction. He had just returned from a three-day dental convention in Colorado and was catching up with all of his appointments.

Wiping the sweat from off of his forehead, Kamal departed from the treatment room. His last patient of the day had just finished paying Julie, his nurse assistant. Kamal glanced down at his cell phone. It was 4:55 pm. He was exhausted and anxious to get home for dinner. Sakina was preparing his favorite meal, lemon-peppered fish, fresh broccoli, and lentil salad.

Kamal began removing his scrub tops and changing back into his regular clothes, when he was interrupted by an overhead page from Julie.

"Dr. Paracha. There are two gentlemen here to see you in the waiting room."

Kamal rolled his eyes and threw down his sweaty scrub top.

" Who on earth wants to see me when its closing time. Didn't they read the sign?" Kamal bitterly complained as he tied his shoes and headed down the short corridor past the reception desk.

"I'm sorry sir, but they insisted," Julie meekly said, seeing the angry expression on Kamal's face.

Kamal took a frustrated deep breath. *"It better be short. I'm exhausted and starving!"*

Kamal walked through the glass door into the waiting room and froze in his tracks, startled by his late evening visitors. Two well-dressed men in black suits with official police badges stood calmly inside the waiting room.

"Good evening, Dr. Paracha. I'm Detective Williams and this is my partner, Detective Ronson. We're both from homicide. We're sorry to disturb you. I know you are closing but we've had a crazy day and were unable to stop by earlier."

Kamal was speechless. He tried to remain calm and collected. Detective Williams reached out to shake Kamal's hand. Kamal hesitated for a moment, but then nervously shook his hand and cleared his throat.

"Homicide?' Kamal blurted out in a startled tone of voice, *" Why do you want to talk to me?"*

Detective Williams turned and gestured toward his partner. *"May we sit down?"*

"Sure," Kamal replied.

Kamal sat down in the chair next to the magazine rack and tried to relax, running the palm of his hand across his black beard.

"As I said, we are from the homicide division. My partner and I are investigating the death of Sheila Watson."

Kamal nervously shifted in his chair, trying to get comfortable.

"I don't know her. Why are you coming to me?"

Detective Williams gave his partner a puzzled look and then quickly refocused his attention back on Kamal.

"Would you mind if we ask you a few questions, Dr. Paracha?"

Kamal took a frustrated deep breath and glanced down at his watch.

"Alright, But I'm in a hurry."

Detective Williams turned on his tablet to take notes.

"Could you tell us your whereabouts on the night of Thursday, June 12 between the hours of 7 and 9:30 pm?"

Kamal sat quietly and thought for a moment, murmuring out loud to himself.

"Thursday, hmm, let's see. I believe that night I was here. I had an emergency case with a patient."

Detective Williams began typing some notes on his tablet.

"Do you remember until what time?"

Kamal stopped and thought for a moment.

"At least 9:00pm."

Detective Williams entered some notes onto the tablet again.

"Well Dr. Paracha, there are two individuals that claimed to have seen you sitting at the bar with Sheila Watson at the Lazy Greco."

Kamal's whole body tightened up. His face turned red with anger.

"Lazy Greco bar!" He blurted out. *"That's impossible!"*

Both detectives remained calm and quiet, carefully studying Kamal's facial reactions.

"First, as I told you. I was here with a patient and second, I'm a Muslim. I don't drink alcohol or go to bars."

Detective Williams pulled a picture out from inside of his coat.

"Do you recognize this woman?"

Kamal had been caught off guard. Detective Ronson observed the startled look on his face. It was a picture of Sheila Watson.

"I don't know this woman!" Kamal insisted, his voice getting louder. *"I've never seen her before in my life!"*

Detective Williams calmly put the picture back inside of his coat.

"Would you be willing to come down to the station and take a polygraph test?"

Kamal inhaled an angry deep breath. His whole body tightened up with anxiety.

"I refuse to answer any more questions. You will have to talk with my attorney."

Detective Williams motioned toward his partner and they both stood up.

"I see. Well, Dr. Paracha. Thank you for your time. We will be in touch."

Kamal abruptly stood up and waited anxiously for the detectives to finally leave. Williams and Ronson walked down the hallway and back out through the front door.

"What do you think?" Detective Ronson curiously asked.

Detective Williams opened up the car door.

"We are going to put Dr. Paracha under 24 hour surveillance and see what his next move will be."

****

When Sakina turned the corner in her Mazda 6 and began driving up the hill to her beach side condo, she was greeted by a small convoy of reporters in their vans. The media had converged on their secluded condo on the hill overlooking the ocean. Sakina was astonished by the sight as she pulled into the driveway circle right behind Kamal's car. Almost immediately, a woman reporter converged on her car as she opened the door.

"Good evening. Are you Mrs. Paracha?"

Sakina nervously closed the car door and stood frozen in her tracks as the lady reporter stood face to face with her.

" What is this all about?" Sakina demanded in a frightened tone of voice.

"I'm Lindsay Burnett, WEYW Channel 19. Are you Sakina Paracha?"

" Yes, I'm Sakina. Why? What do you want?" Sakina nervously answered putting the car keys in her purse.

" What is your reaction to the fact that you husband Kamal has been named by the police as a person of interest in the brutal murder of Sheila Watson?"

Sakina's eyes grew wide with shock.

"Murder?" Person of interest? What?"

"The police went to your husband's dentist office today to question him."

Sakina felt trapped. Camera flashes, clicks, went off in her face. She quickly put her hands in front of her face and began to run toward the front door. Reporters chased after her as she fled.

"Go away! Go away!" Sakina yelled as she nervously turned the keys in the lock, struggling to open the front door.

Once she was safe inside, she immediately locked and slammed the door behind her and fell up against the wall out of breath. At the same moment, Kamal walked in from the kitchen and stared at Sakina with an angry look on his face.

"Kamal. What is going on?" Sakina demanded.

"Nothing," Kamal answered as he headed toward his recliner chair.

"Nothing?" Sakina shouted back. *"They said you are a person of interest in a murder case!"*

"Ignore them, Sakina. Just get dinner. I'm starving!"

Kamal flopped down in his recliner chair and leaned his head back, pretending to be unemotionally affected. Sakina raced over to his chair.

"Kamal. I'm afraid. Why are they here?"

Kamal sat up in his chair, his eyes bulging wide with anger.

"'I told you, nothing!"

Sakina could hear anxious voices outside the door. She ran towards the front door. Kamal leaped out of his chair and immediately grabbed Sakina by her hair. Sakina shrieked and tried to break free of his grip.

"I told you. Forget about them!" Kamal yelled in frustration.

Sakina wrestled with Kamal, struggling to break free from his grip. Losing his patience, Kamal tightened his fist and struck Sakina in her jaw. Sakina screamed in pain and fell backwards, slipping on the rug and striking her head against the couch. She rolled on her side and began moaning out loud. The loud voices from outside the door seemed to fade away as Sakina closed her eyes and fell into unconsciousness.

Kamal walked toward his recliner chair and sat back down. He leaned back and took a long deep breath. The voices from outside the door suddenly became quiet. The media had finally given up for the day.

Sakina had asked too many questions questioning Kamal's authority. Now she lay unconscious on the floor.

Chapter Sixteen

Training Day

Shawn gently touched the dark bruises on Sakina's cheeks with his fingers and then softly kissed her on the forehead. Inside, his soul was raging with anger.

"Today, it's over for Kamal!" Shawn declared as he held Sakina tightly in his arms. Sakina began to quietly sob. *"Today is a new beginning for you, Sakina. He will no longer intimidate you or ever strike you again. I promise you!"*

Shawn held Sakina's face in his hands and gazed deeply into her eyes. Glimpses of fear radiated from Sakina's blue eyes.

"I don't know if I can do this," Sakina confessed.

"Yes you can, Sakina! Today you will become a new person, a warrior, a fighter, an invincible weapon, Kamal's worst nightmare!"

Sakina grinned. A confident smile broke out over her bruised and battered face.

"I love you, Shawn."

Sakina dropped her gym bag by her side and gazed around at the inside of the studio. There were mirrors on every wall so students could practice their kicks and stances and see clearly if they were performing them correctly. There were two punching bags dangling from the ceiling. It was a small but standard sized studio for students to learn the ancient skill of Kung Fu. In preparation for her training, Sakina had reluctantly cut off all of her black flowing hair, so that all that remained was a short, boyish styled haircut. She did this to keep her long black hair from getting in the way of the many kick techniques that she was going to learn.

For comfort and mobility, Sakina was dressed in light, comfortable, silk black jogging pants, which were styled with red-trim on the edges and a white tank top. She wore special black slippers on her feet for comfortability and kicking techniques. Across her forehead, Sakina was wearing a red bandanna. She looked perfect for her first training day.

While Sakina gazed around to inspect the studio, Mr. Wong, her instructor, emerged from his office. He was tall, well built, with short black hair, wearing a similar black uniform like Sakina's.

" Thank you, kind sir, for training Sakina," Shawn happily said as he shook Mr. Wong's hand.

"It is my pleasure, Shawn," Mr. Wong greeted Sakina with a handshake.

" Sakina, I'm Mr. Wong. I'm going to be your instructor. I'm delighted to teach you this powerful ancient art."

*"Thank you, Mr. Wong, "*Sakina meekly replied.

Mr. Wong carefully scrutinized Sakina and looked intently into her eyes.

" Sakina. You have nothing to be afraid of anymore. I will teach you today how to breathe, focus, and relax."

Sakina nodded her head.

" Shawn, if you will excuse us, I think we should get started."

" No problem, " Shawn replied.

Mr. Wong escorted Sakina toward the center of the studio, closer to the mirrors. Sakina glanced at herself in the mirror. She could still see the fear and apprehension in her eyes, inspite of being dressed like a warrior preparing to go to battle. Standing in the center of the studio with Mr. Wong by her side, Sakina continued staring at herself in the mirror. She felt a surge of adrenalin rush through her body. She took a deep breath. A look of fierce determination replaced the fear in her eyes. Every muscle in her body began to tighten up. Sakina began to believe in herself.

"First, I want you to take a few deep breaths and slowly inhale and then on my cue, exhale," Mr. Wong instructed her.

Sakina carefully followed Mr. Wong and inhaled, taking a long, deep breath, holding it for a few moments and then on cue, exhaling it.

"Close your eyes, Sakina and stretch out your arms. Inhale, hold your breath, and then slowly exhale."

Sakina carefully followed Mr. Wong and practiced her breathing, stretching her arms and exhaling on cue. They repeated this exercise together several times.

"Now Sakina, today I want to teach you the basic stances of Kung Fu."

Mr. Wong came to a full, straight stance, with both of his legs together, standing tall and still. Sakina followed him.

"Now first, we're going to learn the "horse stance." Stand straight, breathe, and focus. Now spread your legs open to a horse stance. Keep your back straight. Bend your knees. Now make sure your ankles are in alignment with your knees.

Sakina slowly spread her legs apart. She could feel her muscles become tense. She took a deep breath. There was a slight pain in her muscles as she kept her position and didn't move, allowing her legs to remain stretched. Sweat began to roll down her cheeks.

"Now follow me for now. Don't look at the mirror. Turn your left knee and bend down lower with your right leg, stretching it. Hold that stretch. That's it, Sakina. Good. Now swivel on your heels and turn to your right side."

Sakina could feel her muscles tightening. Pain began to shoot up her legs. She began breathing heavier and sweating more profusely. She realized that her body had been out of shape for far too long.

"Just relax, Sakina. Focus, breathe, hold that stretch and come back to a straight pose."

Sakina brought her legs back together and burst into laughter.

"I'm sorry, sir, but I'm afraid I'm out of shape."

"Don't worry about it, Sakina," Mr. Wong encouraged her, *"I promise you. You will soon become a mighty warrior. You'll see! Today you are like a tiny seed in the ground that one day will burst into a beautiful flower!"*

Mr. Wong stood in front of Sakina and looked intently into her eyes.

"Now I'm going to teach you to punch with power using one of the basic Kung Fu poses."

Mr. Wong took a deep breath and spread his legs apart, coming into horse pose. Sakina did the same. She could feel her muscles heating up from the stretches. She closed her eyes for a moment and breathed slowly, in a relaxed manner. Shooting pains from stretching her muscles distracted her temporarily, but Sakina ignored them and instead concentrated.

"Now. Make a fist with both of your hands and turn them over palms up and relax them by your side."

Sakina carefully followed Mr. Wong.

"You are going to punch one arm at a time. First the right and then the left. Make sure you punch quickly. Make sure your

punches snap from each side of your hips. First the right arm and as you punch from the hip, turn the palm over and then follow quickly with the left arm, until you get into a rhythm. Do you understand?"

"'Yes sir," Sakina confidently replied.

Mr. Wong began punching from the hip in horse stance. First the right arm, quickly snapping and turning the palm over, followed by the left arm. Sakina yelled and released her right arm, turning the palm over, snapping outward for a quick punch and quickly following with her left arm. She found herself getting into a good rhythm, rotating her right arm and then her left arm. Immediately she began to feel the power of her punches, as she stood in horse stance, delivering quick jabs from her hips.

"Good Sakina, Good!" Mr. Wong yelled, impressed by what he was seeing. Mr. Wong looked over toward Shawn and winked his eye with approval. He was encouraged by how quickly Sakina was learning the basics.

" O'kay Sakina. Great punching! Good job!"

Sakina stopped and rested her arms by her side. She smiled with confidence, catching her breath and wiping the sweat from off of her face. Inside, Sakina was feeling confidence beginning to grow, like a seed planted in good soil. She longed for the day that the seed would sprout into a magnificent tall tree.

Next, Mr. Wong demonstrated the various kicks that Sakina would learn in different fighting situations to pulverize her opponent before he could do serious injury to her. Mr. Wong took Sakina to the center of the studio and positioned her close to the punching bag. Then he demonstrated the proper technique for performing a roundhouse kick. Sakina started in horse pose and straddled into a side stance. She concentrated on the punching bag, extending her right foot forward. With her left leg firmly planted behind her, Sakina lifted her right leg, rotated her hip and firmly struck the bag with a snap motion. On her next two attempts, Sakina lost her balance and fell down clumsily on the studio floor. Embarrassed, she shook off her shame and with Mr. Wong's encouragement, tried once again. This time she maintained her balance and firmly struck the punching bag with the side of her foot.

"*Excellent!*" Mr. Wong shouted in approval.

Filled with confidence and determination, Sakina continued to practice the roundhouse kick, successfully maintaining her balance and striking the punching bag swiftly with power and force.

"O'kay, O'kay, enough for today," Mr. Wong announced.

Sakina ran over to Shawn and feel into his arms. Shawn handed her a towel and she began to wipe off her face and hands. Sakina bent over struggling to catch her breath. Every bone and every muscle in her body was screaming out with pain. Yet Sakina didn't care. She felt incredible, powerful and in control! The fear and intimidation that hung over her like a dark cloud when she arrived had melted away. She already felt like a new woman.

"I'm so proud of you Sakina. I knew you could do it and this is only the first lesson!"

Sakina breathed rapidly, struggling to catch her breath.

"I feel great Shawn. I feel like a new woman!"

Shawn tightly hugged Sakina. "*You are my warrior princess!"*

****

It had been a very challenging and exhausting week for Sakina. For two hours a day, she learned kicks, stretching, blocking punches and defense techniques that took her to a whole new level of fighting! Her body and mind had been stretched to the limit, but it didn't bother Sakina. She felt rejuvenated and energized like a brand new woman that had been set free from the shackles of fear and intimidation. A warrior was emerging from deep down in her soul that was now unafraid to face Kamal. For more than twenty years, Sakina had been the victim of abuse and manipulation and now for the first time in her life, she felt like a transformed woman, a warrior replacing a fearful and timid child chained to her fears for a lifetime.

******

Sakina and Shawn flew across the hot sand in their bare feet, jogging at full speed in the scorching afternoon sun. Sakina felt alive and energized. The wind whipped across her face and she felt like the soaring seagulls diving down on the ocean waves as fierce predators searching for food.

"Wow! I can't keep up with you," Shawn complained, lagging farther behind Sakina, and out of breath.

Sakina burst into laughter and finally came to a halt. The ocean waves kissed her bare feet, foaming up and washing over her ankles, as she bent down to catch her breath. Shawn finally arrived at her side, bending over and gasping for breath. Sakina began cooling down with a few deep knee bends and arm stretches. She inhaled the salty ocean air and closed her eyes.

"I feel so good!" Sakina exclaimed.

Shawn put his arms around Sakina's waist and kissed her on the lips. Sakina fell into his arms and laid her head on his shoulder.

"I owe everything to you, dear Shawn!"

Shawn looked deeply into Sakina's eyes.

"No. No, my warrior princess. I've watched you all week go from a timid and fearful girl to becoming a fearless woman of great strength and courage."

Sakina blushed and broke into a grateful smile. She gently kissed the top of Shawn's nose.

"Shawn. You love and support is what I've needed all of my life. You have protected and defended me and treated me like a real woman. If I've accomplished anything, it's because you have stood by me like a real husband."

Tears began to well up in Sakina's eyes. The waves splashed against her bare feet and swirled around her ankles. Shawn gently ran his fingers through Sakina's short black hair.

" Sakina. I love you. I want to heal the scars and pains of your life and be a real husband to you."

Sakina bowed her head, overwhelmed by Shawn's kindness.

" I want this too, but."

"Don't say that, Sakina. I believe it will soon be all over. Then we can be together forever."

Sakina stared intently into Shawn's eyes and laid her head against his chest. .

" This is my dream Shawn. I want this nightmare to be over. I want to be free!"

Shawn and Sakina held each other tight and basked in the hot sunlight savoring the magic of their special moment together on the beach. They didn't want this precious moment to end, but to go on forever. The oceans swirled up against their legs as they passionately kissed, their bodies and souls joined together in an erotic ecstasy.

The warrior princess was still very much like a child, discovering the fiery joy of romance with her angel from heaven.

Chapter Seventeen

A Warrior is born

After six weeks of intensive and exhaustive training, Sakina was finally ready to demonstrate to her trainer, Mr. Wong, what she had learned. Tonight was sparring night. Sakina was dressed in her traditional Kung Fu uniform, white tank top, black silk jogging pants with red trim along the edges, and comfortable slippers. In additional to her traditional uniform, Sakina was wearing padded protective head gear to ensure she didn't suffer serious injuries from kicks and punches.

Shawn stood in the corner of the studio excited and eager to watch Sakina demonstrate her skills. Mr. Wong stepped up to Sakina and warmly smiled. They customarily bowed toward each other.

"Tonight is a very special night, Sakina. Just remember to breathe, focus and relax. Don't worry. I know you will do well. Show me what you've learned. I will be coming at you like a street fighter and a King Fu challenger. Just relax and focus, Ok?"

Sakina nodded her head. She could feel the nervous energy radiating throughout her body like a wild river. She was focused and ready. They once again bowed to each other. Then after a few moments, Mr. Wong lifted his hands and broke out into a fighting stance. Sakina responded, doing the same. She held her hands in front of her chest and focused intently on Mr. Wong's every move. She felt like a cat, stalking her prey. She moved a few steps to the left and immediately Mr. Wong lunged toward her holding his fists in the air with a look of terror in his eyes.

Sakina quickly stepped to her left and immediately evaded his punch. Then with her left hand she blocked his punching hand at his elbow and struck him in the abdomen with her right fist. The blow stunned Mr. Wong, knocking the wind out of him. Sakina quickly returned to her fighting stance, focused, breathing, and relaxed.

Almost immediately, without any warning, Mr. Wong charged toward Sakina again. Without blinking an eye, Sakina alertly stepped to her left and this time, she struck Mr. Wong in the nose with the palm of her right hand, and then added a quick punch to his ribs with her left fist. Mr. Wong stopped to catch his breath and nodded his head in approval.

"Excellent!" He shouted.

Sakina regained her composure and kept her eyes focused on Mr. Wong. Her heart was racing excitedly in her chest. Suddenly out of nowhere, Mr. Wong landed a spinning kick to her head. Sakina, stunned and shaken, fell backwards and landed hard on the studio floor. Sakina immediately regained her composure, rolling quickly to her left as Mr. Wong prepared to jump on top of her.

Sakina leaped up on her feet and fell into a deep knee bended stance and performed a precise sweeping kick and punch to Mr. Wong's ribs. Mr. Wong was astonished at how well Sakina had recovered from being struck by his kick.

Mr. Wong, dazed and confused by Sakina's superior attack, took a few seconds to recover, and then leaped upon her, pushing her up against the wall. He proceeded to apply a choke hold on her just like a street attacker would do. Sakina struggled to break free of Mr. Wong's strong grip. The more that she struggled, the tighter Mr. Wong increased his grip. Panting out of breath, Sakina remembered her techniques. She swiftly grabbed his wrist and forearm and turned her body, bending her knees to loosen the grip. Then she stomped down on Mr. Wong's feet and struck him firmly in the knee with her right foot.

Mr. Wong yelled in pain. Then quickly Sakina stepped behind Mr. Wong and with all of her might and speed, threw him over her leg and struck him in the chest with a two knuckle punch.

"*Bravo! Bravo!*" Shawn screamed and applauded from the corner of the studio.

Sakina stepped back into her fighting stance. Mr. Wong, exhausted and out of breath, stood up and bowed to Sakina. Sakina broke into an excited smile. Mr. Wong walked over to congratulate her and shake her hand.

"I'm very proud of you, Sakina. You have shown me great technique and excellent speed. Tonight in this studio, I'm very happy to announce that a warrior has been born. That tiny seed that was planted deep in the ground so long ago has miraculously sprouted into a beautiful wildflower!"

****

Kamal stepped onto the campus walkway of *Florida Keys Community College.* He had taken the afternoon off to pay a surprise visit to Sakina. For the past two weeks, Kamal noticed she was arriving home much later from her business administration classes. She seemed subdued and strangely quiet around him. Kamal was suspicious she might be meeting another man and this afternoon he was determined to find out.

The front entrance to the business administration building was packed with students holding flyers in their hands. Kamal noticed a group of Muslim men and women engaging in conversations with some of the students. As she stepped up on the concrete steps, a young Muslim woman dressed in a tan burqa stopped him.

"Good afternoon sir. Have you come to attend the lecture and watch the movie?"

Kamal gave the Muslim woman a puzzled look.

"Movie? What movie?"

The Muslim woman handed him a brochure. Kamal looked intently at the brochure and then glanced back at the Muslim woman.

"A young woman has been having weekly lectures in her religion class and showing a film for the past 6 months. The Muslim community has appealed to the College administrator to put a stop to her anti-Islamic rhetoric!"

"I don't' know anything about any movie. I've come here to see my wife!"

"I understand sir. I gave you that brochure so that you would consider signing our petition to stop this film from being shown here on campus."

"Why? What's wrong with it?"

"This woman is spreading lies about Islam and telling students that Muslims are committing honor killings, beating their wives and forcing them to get married against their wills. These are lies and we're asking the public to support us in banning the showing of this film."

Kamal carefully scrutinized the brochure and petition. Suddenly his face was filled with rage. At the bottom of the brochure, he saw Sakina's name as the lecturer for the film.

"Sir. Are you alright?" The Muslim woman asked.

Kamal was both astonished. Rage filled his soul. He felt betrayed! He crumpled up the brochure in his hand and threw it down on the ground and walked away. He quickly ran up the steps and thrust open the entrance door in anger. The hall was filled with students hurrying to their next class. Kamal pushed his way through the crowd desperately searching for Sakina.

Then as he arrived at a classroom halfway down the hall, he froze in his tracks. Just beyond the open door, he spotted Sakina talking with a young male student at the rear of the classroom. Kamal's eyes widened with anger. Sakina was dressed in a tank top and blue jeans. She wasn't wearing her hijab and even worse she was conversing alone with another man.

Feelings of betrayal and anger filled Kamal's soul. He clenched his fists and bit down on his lip. He quickly departed from the classroom and pushed his way through the crowd of students back out to the front entrance. He struggled to control himself as he flung open the glass entrance door. He paused for a moment at the front steps and took an angry deep breath. He knew exactly what he had to do!

Chapter Eighteen

The Stakeout

Detective Williams glanced down at his watch. It was 8:45pm. The orange glow of the sunset streaked across the horizon displaying an awesome sight. Detective Ronson stretched and took a frustrating deep breath. Stakeouts were always boring and agonizing and even veteran detectives hated the assignment of sitting for endless hours in an unmarked vehicle waiting for their suspect to make a move.

Tonight they were staking out Dr. Kamal Paracha. Kamal had refused to take a polygraph test making him a person of interest. Detective Williams had strong suspicions that Kamal was their man, but he needed solid, credible evidence to tie him to the crime scene.

Detective Williams loosened his shirt collar and yawned. He reached down for a sip of coffee.

"Look. There he is!" Ronson blurted out.

Williams almost dropped his sup of coffee. He quickly sat it down and looked through his binoculars. They had parked across the street about one hundred yards from the dental building in a secluded lot, trying to be as obscure as possible. Williams followed Kamal in his binoculars. Kamal was dressed in a blue-striped shirt and brown cacki pants. He stopped to take his keys out of his pocket and open the door of his shiny 2013 black Mercedes Benz.

"Looks like the dentist is going out for a night on the town," Williams remarked as he stalked him with his binoculars.

Kamal started the engine of his Benz. Detective Williams turned the key in the ignition. The engine roared as Kamal backed out of the parking lot and exited onto Duvall Street. After waiting a few seconds, Detective Williams turned on the headlights and carefully followed behind the Benz at a good safe distance so as not to arouse suspicion.

The Black Benz whizzed down Duvall Street. The unmarked cop car kept up with Kamal as he came to a halt at a stop light.

" Wonder where he's headed?" Ronson asked in a curious tone of voice.

" We're about to find out," Detective Williams replied, stepping on the accelerator as the stoplight changed to green.

The Black Benz streaked down Duvall Street. Kamal liked to push his Benz over the speed limit, dodging in and out of traffic, making it challenging for Detective Williams to keep up with him.

Finally the Black Benz made a right turn into the parking lot of *The Full Moon bar and grill.* Kamal drove to the rear of the lot and quickly parked his car. Detective Williams watched carefully from a distance and waited for Kamal to leave his vehicle. As Detective Williams turned into the parking lot, he glanced over toward Ronson with a sarcastic grin on his face.

" Well. We just caught the good dentist in another lie. Remember he said, " I'm a Muslim. I don't go to bars!"

Kamal walked through the front door of the *Full Moon Bar & Grill.* The sound of tvs playing loudly and the intense chatter of people's conversations, greeted his ears. He stopped for a moment to pull his sunglasses down over his eyes to conceal his identity. Kamal gazed around at the tables. It was packed for a Thursday evening. Waitresses were busy taking orders, bus boys were cleaning tables, and the band had arrived to set up their equipment. Kamal looked around the bar. A tall, slender woman with beautiful long black flowing hair was sitting by herself. A perfect opportunity presented itself for Kamal. He slowly walked forward for a closer look. The woman was dressed in a jet black short skirt, wearing black fish net hose and silver isotoners. Kamal drew closer. She was wearing heavy eye shadow and make up with deep red lipstick. To Kamal, she was a goddess, petite, sexy, everything he desired in a woman. He sat down next to her at the bar, relaxed and casual. The goddess was in her own world, quiet, absorbed in thought, and smoking a cigarette, unconcerned and unaffected by her surroundings.

"I'll have a margarita," Kamal told the bartender.

The "goddess" suddenly awakened from her own private world and turned toward Kamal. She had deep blue eyes just like Sakina and a provocative curious smile. Kamal slowly turned toward the woman.

"May I buy you a drink?"

The "goddess" exhaled smoke from her cigarette and remained quiet for a few moments.

"Sure," she answered, *" Why not?"*

"What a sexy, smooth voice," Kamal thought to himself. He reached into his pocket and helped her light another cigarette. The "goddess" inhaled deeply and blew out the smoke.

"Thanks."

The bartender brought the young lady a margarita and sat it down in front of her.

" What's your name?" the goddess asked.

Kamal relaxed in his bar stool.

"Kamal."

"I'm Tabitha."

Kamal smiled at Tabitha underneath his sunglasses. He scrutinized every inch of Tabitha's body, her beautiful eyes, her gorgeous face, perfect breasts, wonderful legs.....

Tabitha took a long sip of her margarita and then stirred it.

"Never seen you here before, Kamal."

"First time."

Tabitha relaxed and began brushing her long black hair.

"What do you do for a living, Kamal?"

"I'm a dentist."

Tabitha smiled and opened her mouth wide.

"I've been a good girl, Kamal. I take care of them."

They both laughed together.

" What do you do?" Kamal asked.

"I'm a massage therapist."

Kamal took a deep relaxing breath.

"Nice."

Tabitha shifted around in her bar stool and faced Kamal.

"I like to help people relax, help them enjoy their day, relieve their stress, make them feel good again."

Kamal nodded his head in agreement and took a drink of his margarita. Then he turned and gazed at Tabitha.

"I was married once, but my man was too possessive of me. He was abusive, didn't want me to work. I told him, Carl, I am a woman. You don't tell me what to do. I live in America. Here women are free to be anything they want to be."

Suddenly, it was if an alien force had seized control of Kamal's mind. The words of Tabitha being a free woman sent a tormenting pain through his mind. Kamal's whole body tightened up. His hand began to shake. He tried to compose himself. Now when he looked in Tabitha's blue eyes, he no longer saw a goddess or a sexy woman. Instead he saw a rebellious whore, a slut, a woman who refused to submit to a man. Tabitha no longer was beautiful or attractive to him. She was now a monster, an ogre, someone worthy of death.

Tabitha watched Kamal's face and demeanor change and transform before her eyes. She watched his hand nervously shaking with rage. Kamal tried to control himself. Suddenly the glass slipped from his hand and broke into pieces on the floor.

The broken glass startled Tabitha. She immediately became confused and afraid. Grabbing her purse, she quickly left the bar and ran toward the women's restroom. The bartender carefully watched the drama unfold. Kamal felt trapped. He quickly laid down a twenty dollar bill on the bar and headed toward the front door. It was the first time he had panicked, but he couldn't risk being seen or identified.

Detective Williams watched with great interest as Kamal left the bar without a woman tonight.

"Something must have gone wrong tonight," Williams observed, *"Let's follow him home and see what he does next."*

Chapter Nineteen

The Confrontation

Sakina walked out the front door of her parent's condo on the beach. In just a few short weeks, the condo would become their permanent home. On Monday, Akbar and Ayesha would return home to Pakistan to take care of some business and then a month later return permanently. Kamal had purchased the beautiful condo as part of a plan for them to apply for citizenship in the United States. Kamal and Sakina's parents shared a special connection with each other. They both shared the exclusive "Pakistani" worldview of family honor and male superiority. Now with the revelation that her parents would be living only a" walk on the beach away" from her home, Sakina felt hopelessly trapped. She desperately wanted a way out and was tired of being chained to a lifestyle of fear and abuse.

It was only a short walk to her condo. She had just finished a productive session with Mr. Wong at the Kung Fu studio. Sakina was exhausted and hungry. Kamal told her earlier he would be late again coming home. That was fine with her. She craved her time alone to relax and forget about her life for a few hours.

The sky was ablaze with orange and purple bursts of color dancing over the horizon. Sunset had fallen in Key West. Sakina marveled at the beautiful horizon as she briskly walked along the shoreline. The ocean breeze filled her lungs with fresh salty air. Sakina breathed in the smell of the ocean. It was an experience she never tired of. The ocean was her friend, an escape from the stress of life, a refuge she could hide away in for a few minutes every day.

Sakina ascended up the hill and arrived at the edge of the cliff which had a breathtaking view of the ocean below. Turning the key, Sakina unlocked the back door. It felt good to be home. Closing the door behind her, she walked into the dark living room to draw back the curtains and enjoy an awesome view of the sunset.

As she walked toward the bay windows, suddenly she was startled by a burst of light. Sakina froze. It was Kamal, sitting in his recliner chair, turning on the lamp beside him.

"I thought-" Sakina nervously stuttered.

"You thought I was still at work," Kamal interrupted.

The look in Kamal's eyes took Sakina's breath away. His black eyes were filled with rage. They had a penetrating and confronting look in them. For a brief moment, fear began to seize her emotions, but Sakina quickly suppressed them realizing a confrontation was about to happen. Sakina decided to remain absolutely quiet and not answer Kamal. That way she would be in total control of her emotions.

Kamal's eyes were fixed intently on Sakina. She watched him began to tightly clench his fists.

"You have disgraced and dishonored me. I know all about what you do every day at college," Kamal declared, his voice filled with anger and disgust.

Sakina took a deep breath. She prepared herself for battle.

"That filthy film that attacks Islam. You have poisoned the minds of students with your lies!" Kamal's voice grew louder with every word.

Suddenly he chuckled and tilted his head back.

"Look at you. All dressed up in some silly Kung Fu outfit," Kamal broke into laughter for a brief moment and then his face was transformed back into that of a raving lunatic.

Kamal slowly stood up. Sakina slowly retreated back a few steps. Her mind began implementing everything that she had learned. She began focusing and then breathing and most importantly relaxing. She stretched out into warrior pose and raised both of her hands up in front of her chest, preparing to fight.

Kamal slowly walked toward her and then stopped. Sakina could see his fists tightly clinched at his side. His eyes penetrated her with the stare of a mad man, a man possessed with uncontrollable rage and anger.

"I have no choice but to kill you! You have dishonored me. You have dishonored the family. You are a slut, a whore, and a traitor!"

Sakina slowly backed up, holding her fighting stance. She quickly assessed her surroundings. A surge of adrenalin filled every fiber of her being. She focused on every part of Kamal's body, absolutely fearless and prepared for his next move. Kamal's eyes bulged wide with anger. Beads of sweat rolled down his cheeks.

He lunged toward Sakina with both hands open, ready to pounce on her. Immediately Sakina stepped to her right side, evading him, and instantly blocked his punch at his elbow and then as swift as the strike of a serpent, Sakina struck Kamal's nose with the palm of her right hand.

Kamal was stunned! He yelled out in pain, grabbing his nose. Drops of blood oozed out from his nostrils. He stood completely still, his hands shaking as he looked down at the blood in his palms. He was astonished!

Quickly composing himself, Kamal once again charged towards Sakina, letting out a fierce yell and throwing an angry punch at her head. Sakina once again quickly stepped out of the way to avoid his punch. Kamal had missed and was staggering off balance. Without wasting a second, Sakina lifted up her right leg, rotating her hip and with a lightning fast snap motion, landed a fierce roundhouse kick in the center of Kamal's chest.

Kamal immediately fell backwards, crashing over the living room table and landing on his back. Sakina quickly returned to her fighting stance, prepared for Kamal to strike again. Sakina was sweating and shaking, her adrenalin rushing through her body. As fear tried to grip her, she immediately suppressed it and stayed focused, waiting for Kamal to get back up.

Moaning and groaning, Kamal staggered to his feet, brushing off the broken pieces of the table that lay scattered all over the floor. He looked at Sakina with a death stare, humiliated that she had crippled him, but now determined to kill her! Kamal rose up with fire and rage in his eyes.

"You bitch," He yelled, shaking his fist at her, *"I'm going to kill you!"*

Quickly he grabbed the lamp from off of the table and with a rage of anger hurled it at Sakina's face. Sakina tried desperately to move out of the way, but part of the lamp grazed her arm. She yelled in pain as the lamp crashed on the floor next to her. Feeling confident and in control, Kamal rushed toward Sakina in her dazed condition. He pressed both of his hands around her throat, putting her in a choke hold.

Sakina gasped for breath and struggled to break free. Kamal crashed her up against the wall. A picture fell off the wall and shattered into pieces on the floor. Kamal's strength was enormous. His grip seemed impossible to break! Sakina was feeling weak and tired. Suddenly her instincts kicked in from training. She stomped down on Kamal's shoes with both of her feet.

Kamal screamed in pain. Sakina then struck his knee cap with her right foot. Kamal loosened his grip, recoiling in pain. With all of her strength, Sakina grunted and broke free. She immediately stepped behind Kamal and threw him across her leg. His body slammed down on the floor.

Kamal laid still, stunned and shocked that Sakina was so strong and fast. He quickly recovered, wiping the blood and sweat from off of his face. Sakina quickly returned to her fighting stance and bent down low, holding her fists in front of her face.

Then without warning, Kamal pulled a knife from out of his pocket and held it in front of her face. His eyes were bulging in anger. His face was covered in sweat and blood. Sakina slowly backed up as Kamal inched forward holding the shiny knife tightly in his right hand, threatening to stab her at any second. Their eyes were riveted on each other. Kamal was determined to kill Sakina, stalking her every move and body gesture.

Then in desperation, Kamal lunged forward to stab and immediately Sakina stepped out of the way of the blade, firing a lightning fast punch to his head. Kamal was stunned. He began to fall backwards. Sakina swiftly grabbed his elbow and disarmed him.

Kamal collapsed on the floor near the broken table. Sakina kicked the knife away from his body, when suddenly Kamal grabbed her ankle. Sakina had been caught off guard. Stunned and out of breath, Kamal managed to grab a broken wooden table leg in his hand. He leaped up and struck Sakina in her back.

Falling face down on the floor next to the broken table, Sakina screamed, withering in pain. Her back and neck felt paralyzed. She struggled to stay conscious. It was as if the floor had been pulled out from underneath her and she had fallen through! Sakina moaned. She felt helpless.

Kamal stood above her gasping for breath. He began chuckling. He felt victorious. Sakina rolled over on her back. She could see his hideous eyes staring at her from above. Kamal reached into his pocket and pulled out a glass vial. Sakina gasped in horror. Unless she acted immediately, she would be dead. If Kamal succeeded in pouring acid all over her face, her fate would be sealed. The room seemed to spin. Her eyes struggled to focus, the images began to blur.

Then Sakina heard a voice from deep down inside of her.

"Sakina. You will not become another statistic. I won't let you become another honor killing statistic!"

"Shawn! Shawn!" Sakina muttered out loud.

Then Sakina heard another voice in her spirit. It was Mr. Wong.

"Sakina. Remember you are invincible! You cannot be defeated!"

A tiny trickle of adrenalin and energy began to surge through her body. Strength began to return to her legs and inner courage and fearlessness once again filled her soul. A blaze of light seemed to fall all around her.

Quickly and instinctively, Sakina rolled over to her left and leaped up on her feet. She immediately fell into her fighting stance and with a fierce yell, she lifted her right knee up, bending it and fired a body crushing side kick into the center of Kamal's chest.

Kamal plummeted backwards with the acid contents in the glass vial spilling all over his face. He yelled in agony, releasing a hideous scream from the depths of his soul and collapsed backwards on the floor, withering in pain. Sakina bent down, agonizing in pain, gasping for breath. She began to weep bitterly for a few moments and then grabbed her cell phone to call 911 and then Shawn.

****

The sound of sirens shattered the cool summer night in Key West. The EMT'S arrived with the police. Sakina led them into the condo to where Kamal was laying. The police took a lengthy statement from Sakina.

Shawn quickly arrived and hurriedly parked the car behind one of the ambulances. Sakina ran excitedly towards Shawn and fell into his waiting arms.

"*Sakina! Sakina! What happened? Are u ok*?" Shawn excitedly asked holding Sakina tightly in his arms, grateful that she was alive.

Out of the corner of her eye, Sakina noticed Akbar and Ayesha rushing towards her. They had seen the lights and heard the sirens and had raced over from their beach condo.

"*Sakina. What's going on?" What happened*?" Ayesha asked with a desperate cry in her voice.

Sakina composed herself and walked toward her parents.

"*Who is that man? What's going on, Sakina*?" Akbar demanded.

Sakina took a deep breath and stared intently into her father's eyes.

"*Kamal tried to kill me!"*

"What? What are you talking about?" Akbar shouted in disbelief.

"*The man you have favored over me. The man that you forced me to marry, father, tried to kill me tonight!"*

Ayesha cupped her hands over her mouth.

"*Sakina! Oh no, not Kamal!"*

"*Yes, Kamal!"* Sakina shouted back in tears. Shawn put his arm back around Sakina.

"Father, for over 20 years you have controlled my life, but you have abused me for the last time. You forced me to marry a man that I didn't love. For 9 years Kamal has made me his prisoner, made me his slave, but after today, no more, father, no more!"

Akbar had a stunned expression on his face.

"I did what was best for you, Sakina."

Sakina drew closer to her father and stared at him face to face.

"Father, today I am no longer Kamal's prisoner. I am no longer your prisoner. You are no longer in control of my life. I am! From now on Father, I will decide. I will make the choices for my life, not you!"

Akbar's face had a shameful look on it. Sakina tightly squeezed Shawn's hand.

"Father. I have found a man who loves me, defends me, and treats me like a real woman. I want you to meet Shawn. Shawn is a real man."

Sakina laid her head against Shawn's shoulder.

"Father. I'm going to marry Shawn. He will be the husband to me that Kamal never was."

Ayesha dropped her head in shame and tears. Akbar looked away in pride and disgust. He refused to look Sakina in her eyes.

"One more thing, father. I have discovered a God who loves me unconditionally and calls me his daughter, not his slave. I am going to become a Christian!'

Akbar shook his head and walked back toward his wife. Sakina looked up into Shawn's eyes with absolute joy.

"Shawn, I love you and will be so honored to become your wife. You have given me the keys to unlock the prison cell that I've been in all of my life."

Shawn gently kissed Sakina on her forehead and held her tightly in his arms.

Sakina was a survivor. She had won the death match of her life and emerged born again! She would not become another honor killing statistic. Tonight she would walk in freedom for the first time in over 20 years, no longer a prisoner of her culture.

Some final thoughts.......

Unfortunately there are not many *Sakinas* who survive! Sakina was fortunate to have a man who was committed to her well-being and loved her unconditionally. Shawn stood by her side and refused to allow her to become another statistic. This story has a happy ending, but for thousands of Pakistani women, their story does not end happily. Their stories end with being buried alive, stabbed to death, attacked with acid or stoned to death. Reality can be very cruel and very bitter to accept.

My motivation to write this book is based on a real life experience. One day about two years ago, I met a young Pakistani born girl on Twitter who was impressed by my support of Iranian women. She invited me to a showing of the "Honor Diaries" film at the university she attended. My friend (I cannot mention her name for security reasons) explained that she was a human rights activist, but that she had to do it secretly for fear of her parents finding out. She lived near the university and when she returned back home for the day, she had to change her clothes back to what women wore in Pakistan to please her father. My friend also explained to me that she was the victim of an arranged marriage and her husband was currently living back in Pakistan, awaiting his Visa clearance. One day, he was coming to the United States and she would have to submit to his rule over her.

During one of our last visits, my friend told me she was going to take martial arts classes and do her best to not become another statistic when her husband finally came to the United States. That was the last conversation that I had with my friend. My friend was a guest on my radio program several times and shared her convictions as a Muslim who was unafraid to break the silence and speak out. She was a courageous champion for human rights that refused to stay silent. I admired and respected her very much. She is in the battle for her life. Although I haven't heard from her in a few months, I keep her always in my thoughts and prayers.

This is the reason I wrote this book, to be a voice for Pakistani women. I know that she would be pleased with the book that I've written. In one of the last conversations that we had, she asked me to write her story if anything happened to her. I hope and pray that I never have to write that story.

Randy L. Noble

August 2015

If you wish to contact the author……..

Email me: rnoble1065@sbcglobal.net

Facebook page: Randy L. Noble

Twitter: randyforiran

Blog: Thecrossinthedesert.blogspot.com

Previous book by *Randy L. Noble*

Beyond the Veil: Where we can see God clearly

Shining Star: A light in the darkness of Iran

The promise: We will meet again

Driven by the wind: the calling of Tara

The Rose of Nowruz: dreams of hope and freedom

Tears in a bottle: seeing through their eyes

Beauty from the ashes: the promise fulfilled

The Cross in the desert: speaking hope and freedom to Iran

Printed in Great Britain
by Amazon

56290727R00108